# OFFICIATING FOOTBALL

A publication for the National Federation of State High
School Associations Officials Education Program

Developed by the
American Sport Education Program

Human Kinetics

**Library of Congress Cataloging-in-Publication Data**

National Federation of State High School Associations Officials Education Program.
   Officiating football : NFHS Officials Education Program / developed by the American Sport Education Program.
      p. cm.
   Includes index.
   ISBN 0-7360-4758-1 (soft cover)
   1. Football--Officiating--United States.   2. School sports--United States.   I. American Sport Education Program.   II. Title.
   GV954.35.N38 2005
   796.332'3--dc22

                                                                                              2004022465

ISBN: 0-7360-4758-1

Copyright © 2005 by Human Kinetics Publishers, Inc.

All rights reserved. Except for use in a review, the reproduction or utilization of this work in any form or by any electronic, mechanical, or other means, now known or hereafter invented, including xerography, photocopying, and recording, and in any information storage and retrieval system, is forbidden without the written permission of the publisher.

The Web addresses cited in this text were current as of November 2004, unless otherwise noted.

**NFHS Officials Education Program Coordinator:** Mary Struckhoff; **Project Consultant:** Jerry Diehl; **Project Writer:** Jeff Barr; **Acquisitions Editors:** Renee Thomas Pyrtel and Greg George; **Developmental Editor:** Laura Floch; **Assistant Editor:** Mandy Maiden; **Copyeditor:** Bob Replinger; **Proofreader:** Kathy Bennett; **Indexers:** Robert and Cynthia Swanson; **Graphic Designer:** Andrew Tietz; **Graphic Artist:** Sandra Meier; **Photo Manager:** Dan Wendt; **Cover Designer:** Jack W. Davis; **Photographer (cover):** Dan Wendt; **Photographers (interior):** Dan Wendt; photos on pages 1, 6, 11, 51, 121, 125, 131, 135, 137, 142, and 145 © Human Kinetics; **Art Manager:** Kareema McLendon; **Illustrators:** Argosy and Kareema McLendon; **Printer:** United Graphics

We thank the University of Illinois at Urbana-Champaign for assistance in providing the location for the photo shoot for this book.

Copies of this book are available at special discounts for bulk purchase for sales promotions, premiums, fundraising, or educational use. Special editions or book excerpts can also be created to specifications. For details, contact the Special Sales Manager at Human Kinetics.

Printed in the United States of America

10   9   8   7   6   5   4   3   2   1

**Human Kinetics**
Web site: www.HumanKinetics.com

*United States:* Human Kinetics
P.O. Box 5076
Champaign, IL 61825-5076
800-747-4457
e-mail: humank@hkusa.com

*Canada:* Human Kinetics
475 Devonshire Road Unit 100
Windsor, ON N8Y 2L5
800-465-7301 (in Canada only)
e-mail: orders@hkcanada.com

*Europe:* Human Kinetics
107 Bradford Road, Stanningley
Leeds LS28 6AT, United Kingdom
+44 (0) 113 255 5665
e-mail: hk@hkeurope.com

*Australia:* Human Kinetics
57A Price Avenue
Lower Mitcham, South Australia 5062
08 8277 1555
e-mail: liaw@hkaustralia.com

*New Zealand:* Human Kinetics
Division of Sports Distributors NZ Ltd.
P.O. Box 300 226 Albany
North Shore City, Auckland
0064 9 448 1207
e-mail: blairc@hknewz.com

GV
954.35
.N38
2005

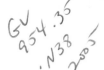

# CONTENTS

WITHDRAWN
KELLY LIBRARY
Emory & Henry College
Emory, VA 24327

# PREFACE

Officials are an essential part of high school football in this country. But how do officials come to know their stuff, to excel at their craft? How do they keep all the rules and mechanics straight throughout every game and every season? Educational tools and reference materials—such as this book—are useful in helping officials not only learn their craft but also stay sharp. *Officiating Football* is a key resource for those who want to officiate football games at the high school level. The mechanics you'll find here are developed by the National Federation of State High School Associations (NFHS) and used for high school football throughout the United States.

We assume that you know at least a little about football but perhaps not much about officiating it. Or you might know plenty about both. In any case, the objective of *Officiating Football* is to prepare you to officiate games, no matter what your level of experience. More specifically, this book will

- introduce you to the culture of officiating football,
- tell you what will be expected of you as a football official,
- explain and illustrate the mechanics of officiating football in detail,
- show the connection between the rules of football and the mechanics of officiating it, and
- serve as a reference for you throughout your officiating career.

*Officiating Football* covers officiating basics, officiating mechanics and specific play situations. In part I you'll read about who football officials are and what qualities you'll find in a good football official. Part I also completely describes game responsibilities, including pregame and postgame duties. Part II, the meat of the book, describes positioning, mechanics and responsibilities in four- and five-person systems, all in careful detail. You'll find these mechanics chapters well organized and amply illustrated. Part III highlights some key cases from the *NFHS Football Case Book* and shows how you, the official, apply the rules in action.

*Officiating Football* is a practical how-to guide approved by the NFHS. This book is also the text for the *NFHS Officiating Football Methods* online course, which also has been developed and produced by the American Sport Education Program (ASEP) and the NFHS. To find out how you can register for the online course, visit www.ASEP.com.

# NFHS Officials Code of Ethics

Officials at an interscholastic athletic event are participants in the educational development of high school students. As such, they must exercise a high level of self-discipline, independence and responsibility. The purpose of this code is to establish guidelines for ethical standards of conduct for all interscholastic officials.

- Officials shall master both the rules of the game and the mechanics necessary to enforce the rules, and shall exercise authority in an impartial, firm and controlled manner.
- Officials shall work with each other and their state associations in a constructive and cooperative manner.
- Officials shall uphold the honor and dignity of the profession in all interactions with student-athletes, coaches, athletic directors, school administrators, colleagues and the public.
- Officials shall prepare themselves both physically and mentally, shall dress neatly and appropriately, and shall comport themselves in a manner consistent with the high standards of the profession.
- Officials shall be punctual and professional in the fulfillment of all contractual obligations.
- Officials shall remain mindful that their conduct influences the respect that student-athletes, coaches and the public hold for the profession.
- Officials shall, while enforcing the rules of play, remain aware of the inherent risk of injury that competition poses to student-athletes. When appropriate, they shall inform event management of conditions or situations that appear unreasonably hazardous.
- Officials shall take reasonable steps to educate themselves in the recognition of emergency conditions that might arise during the competition.

# KEY TO DIAGRAMS

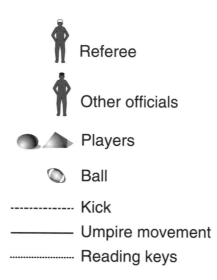

Referee

Other officials

Players

Ball

-------------- Kick

——————— Umpire movement

...................... Reading keys

# PART I

# FOOTBALL OFFICIATING BASICS

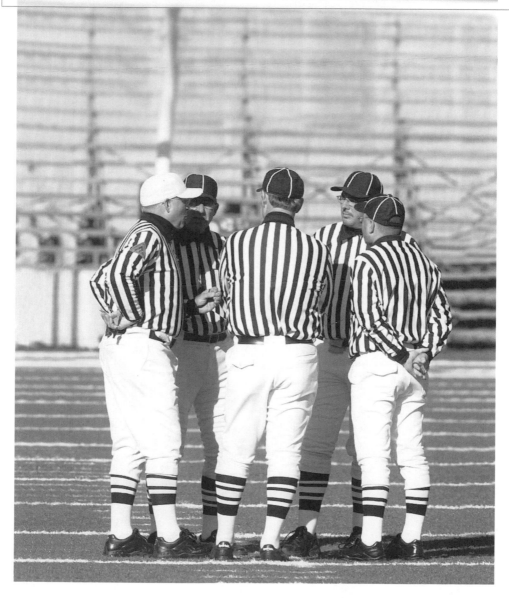

# CHAPTER 1

# INTRODUCTION TO FOOTBALL OFFICIATING

The fact that you have opened this book is a strong indicator that you are interested in becoming a high school football official. If you are already an official, then you might be interested in improving your understanding of what it takes to become a better official. In this chapter, you will find answers to some basic questions about what it means to be a high school football official.

What is the purpose of officials in football? Who are football officials? What makes a good football official? What tools are available to make a football official more effective? What are the unique aspects and systems of officiating football in high school as opposed to youth, college and the professional level? And what is the role of state associations and the National Federation of State High School Associations (NFHS)? If these questions sound like a lot to tackle, they are. The job of a high school football official is complex and important, but these questions have direct answers for the prospective official willing to invest the time to find them.

The NFHS Football Rules Code allows competition to be conducted in an equitable, exciting and interesting manner while at the same time specifically prohibiting unnecessary roughness, unfair tactics and unsporting conduct. If the action of the players does not conform to the rules, the potential values of the game experience will be compromised. This is where you come in.

Game officials must accept the responsibility of enforcing the letter, as well as the spirit, of the rules promptly and with consistency. Therefore, knowledge and understanding of the rules are necessary. You'll need to make decisions so quickly that they come by reflex. How can you prepare yourself for making these decisions? Learn the rules, understand them and continue to study them. You should also learn as much as you can about how the rules apply in the many and varied game situations. The fundamentals should become second nature, and correct interpretations should be virtually automatic.

# Purpose and Philosophy

A thorough knowledge of the rules is important, but it is not enough to guarantee the competency of an official. Besides complete mastery of the rules, officials must have a good knowledge of human nature and the ability to control situations as they arise. At times, the emotions of players, coaches and crowds run high, and the official must control personal emotions and provide necessary leadership.

Rules define the officials' duties and responsibilities, and *Officiating Football* will help you carry out those duties. But experience is the best teacher when it comes to learning how to make instant decisions, how to adjust to emergencies, how to show poise and control temper, and how to be courteous and considerate yet firm and decisive. Along with learning the rules of the sport, you must become familiar with the mechanics required of each member of a football officiating crew. If you know your mechanics, you'll be in the right position to make the call; if you're in the right position, making a judgment is that much easier.

As an official, you are certainly expected to exercise good judgment in applying the rules. There is no magic formula, but at a minimum it takes hard work and hustle. Although officiating is an avocation, it requires dedication. Players who have practiced long hours deserve competent officials who not only understand the rules but also administer them consistently and fairly. To command respect and keep the game moving, you must make quick and positive decisions. If you hesitate or are timid, you are likely to lose the confidence of those around you in your ability as an official. This perception could jeopardize your control of the game. You'll need all the self-confidence you can muster. People may question your decisions from time to time—that is part of the game—but if you display confidence, they will more readily accept your judgments.

## Courage and Consistency

A basic requirement for all sports officials is courage. When you see an infraction or violation, you must make the call promptly. The protection and welfare of the players are paramount. With this there can be no compromise—especially in the high-contact sport of football. You must be consistent in your calls, never allowing the score of the game, your future relationship with a school or coach, or pressure from fans, coaches or players to cause bias. To build your reputation of competence as an official in your area, you must resist these pressures and intimidations.

You can use several techniques to keep pressure and tension to a minimum during a contest. One powerful technique is known as preventive officiating. Practicing preventive officiating means taking opportunities to prevent fouls and conflicts from happening. Good officials, through the use of actions and words, can often prevent certain fouls from occurring. Like a traffic officer at a busy intersection who keeps traffic moving without making arrests, a competent official keeps the game moving by using accepted methods to maintain a safe contest while ensuring competitive fairness. But you must be able to draw the line between preventive officiating and coaching. If you tell a coach, "Get that player out so I don't have to throw him out," you are dictating playing time to a coach, and you have unacceptably crossed the line. Yet a well-placed, calm remark to the coach such as, "Coach, I could use some help with number 24" might prevent unnecessary conflict.

Discussing with the coaches before the game any unusual plays that they may use, particularly those in which you might be in the way, is a useful preventive technique. Routine checking of game equipment and counting players on every play are critical to successful officiating. Helping players line up following a safety or for other free kicks also is an acceptable preventive technique.

You can set the tone by putting a stop to derogatory comments between players. Avoid talking to players, however, while the ball is live or when it is about to become live. Remind captains that it is their responsibility to help stop and prevent problems during a game by directing players to abstain from baiting, taunting or similar practices.

During time-outs, call the captains' attention to the number of time-outs they have remaining. Be certain that both coaches know when they have taken their legal limit of time-outs. Check with other officials regarding this matter during every time-out.

Sounding the whistle sharply contributes to a reduction of fouls. Calling to the players by saying, "Play's over," "That's all," "That's enough" or "Don't hit him" after the ball is dead either inbounds or out of bounds will frequently deter a player from making late contact and thereby fouling. When a kick goes out of bounds, all officials can call to players, "Stand up, the ball is out of bounds."

## Communication

Communication with other members of the crew is essential. The smooth conduct of the game depends on how well the officiating crew on the field works with the timekeeper and members of the line-to-gain crew. The field-clock operator must attend the pregame conference with the field officials so that he or she is completely aware of and understands the signals. Officials explain the procedures for the end of a period or the game at that time. The linesman meets with the line-to-gain crew before the game to review proper procedures. These assistant officials

Communication between members of an officiating crew is essential.

are part of the officiating team. They contribute to smooth game administration, and officials should treat them as an important part of game
management.

Authorized signals provide the only means for the crew of officials to
communicate with coaches, assistant officials and fans. The signals are
dignified, informative and meaningful. Poorly executed or unauthorized
signals confuse the situation and impair communication. The manner
in which an official gives the signal determines, at least to some degree,
the level of acceptance by players, coaches and fans.

Your appearance as an official, another aspect of communication,
greatly affects the attitude of coaches, players and fans. If you are dressed
sloppily, you may sense a lack of respect. Careless dressing definitely
affects the way your decisions are accepted on the field. If you wear the
proper uniform and have a neat appearance, you will be more likely to
receive respect.

The physical condition of an official is another important part of appearance. Officials who act in a professional manner, move quickly from one position to another and have the stamina to last throughout the game will have more success than officials who do not possess those qualities. Officiating is strenuous work. To meet the challenge, you should have a thorough annual physical examination and maintain your physical conditioning. If you are out of condition, more often than not you will do a poor job of officiating simply because you will be unable to cover the play. Be sure to eat properly on a regular basis and make sure that you are well nourished and well rested before a game.

# What Makes a Good Football Official?

Just as players need a mix of skills to perform well, officials need a range of skills and competencies to be good at their jobs. Sometimes those skills and competencies can seem almost contradictory.

For example, to be a good official, you have to blend into the background in one sense yet at the same time be omnipresent and authoritative. You have to maintain control yet keep the game in the players' hands. In the highly emotional arena of sport, you must keep your head about you while all others are losing theirs.

Inevitably, you will make some mistakes. No one is perfect. Learn from your mistakes and do your best never to repeat them.

No one said that being a good official was easy. But many good officials are out there, and they got there through careful preparation and dedication to their profession. You can join the ranks of good officials by following the 12 prerequisites for good officiating:

## 1. Keep in shape.

Although it is important that you have an alert, healthy and sound mind, it is equally important that you keep your body agile and strong. Today's athletes are well conditioned, skilled and fast. You need to keep pace with them. Frequently, you'll need to move quickly to get into ideal position. If you aren't physically fit, you're a detriment to the game. Be in good physical shape before the season begins and maintain your conditioning throughout the season.

## 2. Make calls positively and with good timing.

If you're a novice official, be careful about rendering decisions prematurely. Make decisions positively and with good timing, but don't be too hasty in calling a play. After a momentary hesitation to come to a

## Official Uniform

Uniforms should fit properly and be clean and neat. The first impression is important when establishing authority and respect, and nothing has a bigger influence on first impressions than appearance. A sharp, crisp appearance lets coaches, players and fans from both sides know that you take your job seriously. Baggy, unkempt uniforms also make a first impression, one that you probably would rather not make.

The proper attire for a high school football official is:

1. A black-and-white vertically striped, long- or short-sleeved knit shirt shall be worn. The shirts shall have 1-inch stripes, a black knit cuff and a Byron collar. All officials, in a given game, should wear the same type of shirt.

2. Standard, all-white tapered knickers shall be worn with a short overlap below the knee (not more than 4 inches).

3. One-piece stockings with a modified northwestern stripe (1/2 inch white, 1/2 inch black, 1 inch white, 1/2 inch black, 1/2 inch white) are required. The width of the black showing below the knickers should be the same as the wide black band below the striping pattern.

4. Black football shoes with black laces are required. Shoes should be shined before each game.

5. A black baseball-style cap with white piping is required. To aid in identification, the referee shall wear a solid white baseball-style cap.

6. A black leather belt 1 1/4 to 2 inches wide with a plain buckle shall be worn.

7. By state association adoption, a black-and-white vertically striped jacket may be worn during the game.

8. By state association adoption, white officiating shorts (with a 5-inch inseam) may be worn in place of the traditional knickers if the entire crew wears them. If the shorts have loops, a black belt as described earlier is required. All officials, in a given game, are to wear the same type of shorts.

Besides wearing the proper uniform, all officials must have the proper equipment; essentials are a whistle, penalty marker, white beanbag to mark nonpenalty spots, game card, pencil and rubber bands or some device to keep track of the down number. The penalty marker shall be a light gold flag (15 inches by 15 inches) with a middle pouch weighted with sand, beans or some other material. The linesman shall furnish a clipping device for use in measuring first downs.

decision, forcefully make the call. Timidity or extended hesitation indicates lack of confidence. Call all plays with confidence, a practice that you can develop with experience and preparation.

Positive and forceful action does much in getting your call accepted. Cultivate your voice to increase your authority through your spoken word. A strong voice is a valuable asset. Make all calls loudly and clearly so that players of both teams can hear them. Also, make your hand gestures with confidence. A timid hand gesture suggests uncertainty.

### 3. Know the rules.

To be a competent official, you need to know the rules thoroughly. You make some decisions repeatedly, so with experience some calls will come by reflex. Prepare yourself to make decisions effectively in every circumstance through continual study of all possible situations. Fundamentals then become second nature, and correct interpretations become automatic.

Knowing the rules thoroughly requires constant analytical study. As you study the rules, form mental pictures of plays. These mental images will help you recognize situations when they occur during games, and you'll be better prepared to make the correct calls. Remember, if through your calls you show that you don't know the rules, you will lose the confidence and respect of players, coaches and spectators.

### 4. Know the mechanics.

Your knowledge of the rules might be enormous, but if your mechanics are poor you will have a hard time gaining acceptance of your calls. When a crew of officials uses proper mechanics, no play can occur without their being in the desired position to see the play clearly.

You need to master the mechanics, or play coverage, to be successful. First, you must learn proper positions for various situations, and then you need to practice the coverage so that positioning becomes second nature. You should take the best position possible for any given play without being in the way of any player. Look for opportunities to discuss and review position and coverage at clinics and to practice the mechanics, whether you're a novice or a veteran.

### 5. Ignore the fans.

Know that you will be heckled. Every crowd includes some fans who believe that it's not only their right but their duty to insult the officials. Ignore remarks from fans. The same fans who heckle you will lose respect for you if you react to their criticism or indicate that you're aware of their heckling. And when that happens, their criticism becomes more intense. Two traits of good officials are having a deaf ear toward fans and a thick skin impervious to barbs and catcalls.

### 6. Don't draw undue attention to yourself.

Don't be a showboat; execute your duties without flair. When you take care of your responsibilities with dignity and in conformance with accepted signals and procedures, you'll encourage players and spectators to accept your decisions. Being excessively dramatic doesn't accomplish any good purpose, and such actions frequently cause players to lose confidence in the decisions made because it may seem that an actor made them, not an official. Quiet dignity is more effective. Don't be self-important and bossy, but don't tolerate disrespect either.

### 7. Be courteous to players and coaches, but don't fraternize with them.

Be courteous to players and coaches, but avoid visiting with them immediately before, during or after a game (other than in the pregame conference, of course). Never attempt to coach a player, and don't argue with players, coaches or team representatives. Keep your discussions with these personnel brief and businesslike. A dignified attitude will often preclude and prevent an argument.

### 8. Hustle and be alert.

To be successful, you have to hustle and be alert. These closely related characteristics are of critical importance. Move briskly and, when appropriate, urge players to hustle. Keep your head erect and maintain a posture and appearance of one who can properly discharge his responsibility. When the play is ready to begin, you should never have your arms folded.

### 9. Call them as you see them.

Your decision-making skills sharpen with experience. Remember to base your decisions on fact. First, cover the play according to proper procedures and mechanics. Second, and more important, rule on the play exactly as you saw it.

Understand that you will sometimes err in your judgment no matter how conscientious and efficient you are and regardless of your position and rules knowledge. When you make a mistake, simply continue to work to the best of your ability. Being unduly humbled or embarrassed isn't necessary. And never attempt to even it up. Make each call on its own merits.

### 10. Be loyal to your crew members.

Through your actions and, when necessary, your words, endorse and support the decisions of your fellow crew members. Be willing to accept responsibility and don't attempt to shift blame to another member of the

Officials must base their call on the facts and call each play exactly as they saw it happen.

crew. Don't discuss specific decisions made in a game with the media and don't publicly criticize a fellow official.

### 11. Maintain rapport and respect for other crew members.

Have respect for your fellow officials. Friendliness and respect for members of the crew (and for the profession) contribute to confidence in one another. Support your partners throughout the entire contest. When one official requests an opinion from another concerning a play, the opinion should be given courteously to the official requesting it and to him only.

### 12. Don't infringe on the duties of other crew members.

Make a conscientious effort not to infringe on the duties and responsibilities of fellow officials. Extreme embarrassment results when officials make opposing decisions on a play. When officials observe proper mechanics, conflicting decisions should not occur.

## Football Official's Tools

There are several tools that can help you excel as an official. The following are a few examples:

- *The current* NFHS Football Rules Book. Get it, learn it backward and forward and sleep with it under your pillow. Know it as well as you possibly can.
- *Officiating resources.* Use this book and the *Officiating Football Mechanics CD (NFHS Edition),* another product of the NFHS Officals Education Program, which shows animated mechanics, as well as magazines and other resources to aid you in honing your skills.
- *Firsthand experience.* Use every officiating experience to learn, improve, expand your knowledge of the game and extend your ability to officiate.
- *Secondhand experience.* Learn from watching other good officials, either in person or on television. Watch their mechanics, how they comport themselves, how they exercise their authority and how they make their calls. Adapt what is useful to your style.
- *Your crewmates.* Learn from their sometimes differing styles and discuss plays and other related issues after games. Keep each other sharp in this manner.
- *Clinics and workshops.* Attend as many rules clinics as you possibly can. If none are offered in your area, suggest to some veteran officials that they design one of their own. Speak with representatives of schools in your area and develop a workshop or other learning experiences. And don't stop with one clinic or course. Continue to learn throughout your career. Stay sharp. Never become complacent with your learning.
- *A journal.* Use a journal as a self-assessment tool, charting areas for improvement, successes, progress and things learned from each game.
- *Review from others.* Request that a fellow official from your local officials' chapter come watch you during a game and comment on your work.
- *Self-review.* Have a friend videotape a game so that you can review it later.
- *Pre- and postgame meetings.* Meetings before and after games are key learning times for officials, especially beginners. If you're a new official or even if you're a veteran, there's no shame in asking a more experienced official for advice.

# Officiating at the High School Level

Many rules are unique to high school football, so the rules and mechanics included in *Officiating Football* apply specifically to the high school level. Remember that interaction between officials and players is different in high school than it is at any other level. Many high school players are at or near physical maturity, but that doesn't necessarily mean that they are emotionally mature. When you toss in the adrenaline involved during the heat of competition, the emotional balance of a high school player can become delicate. The high school player is a hybrid of a youth player and a player at a higher level of football. When dealing with high school players, keep those unique characteristics in mind.

Another important aspect to remember when studying *Officiating Football* is the application of the four- and five-person crew systems. As a rule, most high school associations require either a four-person or a five-person crew. The explanations of the procedures in *Officiating Football* allow you to make a quick adaptation from one crew size to the other. State associations also are encouraged to adopt mechanics for six- and seven-person crews, but this book does not discuss those adaptations. Six- and seven-person crews are rarely used at the high school level, but if your association is one that employs them from time to time, you obviously must know how to adapt. Chapters 3 and 4 will deal with responsibilities and positioning of four- and five-person crews and how they differ. But a simple explanation of the difference between a four- and five-person crew is this: A four-person crew consists of a referee, umpire, linesman and line judge. A five-person crew comprises those four plus a back judge.

As a high school football official, you'll be part of the NFHS Officials Association, through which you are taking this course. Through your state officials' association, you can receive assignments, attend annual rules meetings to learn new rules and hone your techniques and other skills, and attend clinics throughout the year. Take advantage of your membership in both the NFHS Officials Association and your state organization to continue to learn and develop your skills as an official.

# CHAPTER 2

# Game Procedures and Responsibilities

If you've already officiated football games, you know that many responsibilities go along with the job. If you haven't officiated any games yet, you'll find out soon enough. In this chapter we'll break down the responsibilities of each official on the field in general terms and then get more specific with procedures to use pregame, during the game and at the end of the game.

## Individual Responsibilities

Knowing each official's role and areas of coverage is the starting point for understanding how to officiate football. Let's start with some general guidelines. The referee is the head of the crew and the administrator of the game. The referee signals when the ball is ready for play, gives the infraction signals and generally operates as the CEO on the field. The umpire spots the ball until the referee gives the ready-for-play signal and watches the interior of the line on plays from scrimmage.

The linesman, line judge and back judge in a five-person crew are generally responsible for watching receivers, backs and play "outside the box."

These general guidelines should give you a basic understanding of officials' roles until we cover them in more depth in chapters 3 and 4.

### Basic Positions

As you most likely already know, football is a game of action, but officials must position themselves in order to properly begin a game. Figure 2.1, a and b, illustrates the basic starting positions for four- and five-person crews. Officials should react automatically to assume these positions at the beginning of every play. As the previous play is wrapping up and the ball is being spotted, hustle into position. You should have no need to think, "Where should I be?" Quick, decisive action when getting into position not only helps the flow of the game but also indicates to all involved that you know what you're doing. The following will help you understand the starting positions of each official on plays from scrimmage when operating in a four- or five-person crew:

- *Referee.* On the passing-arm side of the quarterback, approximately 10 to 12 yards deep and at least as wide as the tight end. The referee (R) must be able to view the backs and the tackle on the far side of the field.
- *Umpire.* Three to 8 yards behind the defensive line and between the defensive ends, keeping the snap in full view. The umpire (U) must

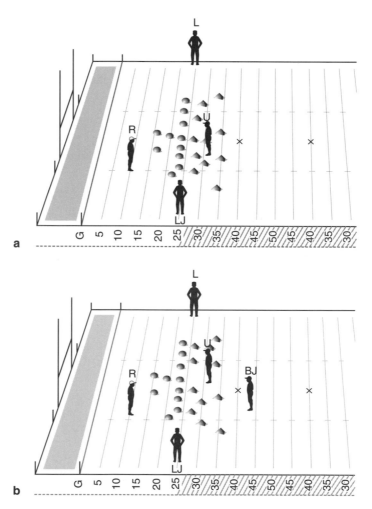

FIGURE 2.1 Basic starting positions for a (*a*) four-person crew and (*b*) five-person crew.

avoid interfering with the vision or movement of defensive backs and should vary position so that players cannot use the umpire as interference.

- *Linesman and line judge.* The linesman (L) and line judge (LJ) are each on opposite sides of the field, straddling the line of scrimmage not closer than 9 yards outside the widest offensive player.

- *Back judge (five-person crew).* Favoring the strong side of the formation, the back judge (BJ) positions himself 15 to 20 yards beyond the line of scrimmage and deeper than the deepest defender.

## Intercrew Communication

Communication—not only during plays but at all times—is essential to the functioning of an officiating crew. Working as a unit is the only way for a crew to be effective. In addition to using the obvious method of constantly talking to each other between plays, officials can communicate in other ways. This is particularly important when they are positioned too far away from each other to be heard. Intercrew communication signals are a universally recognized method of communicating with your crew. They are:

### Double Stakes

Double stakes indicates more than 10 yards to go before a first down, to prevent accidental stopping of the clock. The official should cross his arms in front of his chest, with fists clenched (see figure 2.2).

FIGURE 2.2   Official signaling double stakes.

### Player Count Complete

A fist at shoulder level indicates that 11 players are in the game and that counting of players is complete. The official should hold the clenched fist in front of his body, under his chin at shoulder level (see figure 2.3). The proper signal appears as if the official is in "punching position" with the fist under his chin.

### Protection for Snapper

The referee and umpire rotate their hands in front of the chest to let each other know that the play requires protection for the snapper in accordance with the rules. The official rotates his hands, with fists clenched, at shoulder level in front of his chest (see figure 2.4).

FIGURE 2.3  Official signaling that the player count is complete and the respective team has 11 players.

FIGURE 2.4  Official signaling protection for snapper and fourth-down reminder.

### Unbalanced Line

A hand on the cheek indicates an unbalanced line, triggering other officials to look for ineligible receivers and for the umpire to check for numbering. Officials also use this signal to indicate that two or more players or no players are outside the tackle on the line of scrimmage. The official places one hand, palm flat, on his cheek (see figure 2.5).

FIGURE 2.5    Official signaling an unbalanced line.

### Progress Stopped Inbounds

The official winds the clock twice with the proper winding-arm signal by rotating the hand vertically and then crossing both hands over his head. The official should then stop the clock with the time-out signal (see figure 2.6, a-e). This signal indicates that progress was stopped inbounds and that the first down has been attained.

FIGURE 2.6    (*a-e*) Official signaling progress stopped inbounds.

### Ball Out of Bounds on Last Play

A signal of extending the arms below the waist with the palms toward the sideline and outside the body indicates that the last play was out of bounds and that the clock starts on the snap. This signal is from one official to the referee, and the official should make the call with the arms at the sides, pushed toward the sideline, with the palms facing away from the field (see figure 2.7).

### Backward Pass

One arm extended straight out and parallel to the ground indicates a backward pass has been thrown (see figure 2.8). The referee gives this signal unless the pass comes immediately after the snap, in which case the line judge has the option to signal. No signal is given for a forward pass. Before the snap, the same signal given by the linesman and line judge indicates that the player nearest that official is off the line of scrimmage.

Be sure to learn these basic signals along with the other signals you'll use for calling the game. In addition, you and your crew may develop signals for communicating among yourselves as the need arises.

FIGURE 2.7   Official signaling last play out of bounds.

FIGURE 2.8   Official signaling backward pass.

# Crew Responsibilities

Some state high school athletic associations require a four-person crew; others require a five-person crew. Those that require a four-person crew during the regular season may add a fifth official for state playoffs. The fifth official in all cases is the back judge. The back judge helps on deep coverage during plays from scrimmage, covers action in the middle of the field and is especially helpful on special-teams plays, which stretch the capacity of officials to cover the entire field. As common sense would dictate, a fifth official can only help. Ten eyes obviously can take in more than eight, and five sets of legs can cover more ground than four.

Besides your crew of four or five officials, other "officials"—the clock operator and the line-to-gain crew—are typically on hand at games to help your crew perform your job more efficiently. As an official, you should meet them and review protocol. On most occasions, these people will be strangers to you. Although they aren't formal members of your officiating crew, they are integral performers that can make your job either much easier or much more difficult. Typically, the home team's game administration provides the clock operator and line-to-gain crew. A representative of the visiting team need not serve as a member of the line-to-gain crew.

The game management is required to make available a competent crew to operate the line-to-gain equipment, whether it is the traditional rods and chain or some other measuring device. All members of the line-to-gain crew should have distinctive vests or jackets so that they will be readily recognizable. Ideally, these individuals will be adults. A competent line-to-gain crew is trained in its responsibilities and capable of discharging its various duties. The crew must be alert, agile and responsive to the leadership and direction of the linesman.

### Field-Clock Operator

The electric field-clock operator should follow the direction of the on-field officiating crew. The clock operator attends the pregame conference (as explained later in this chapter) with officials to review the signals and then checks the operation of the scoreboard clock.

Officials should treat this pregame meeting as more than just a formality. Undoubtedly, moments will occur during a game when communication between officials and the clock operator will be necessary to ensure that the time of the game is being monitored correctly. A small discrepancy can alter the outcome of a game. If the clock operator isn't quite sure what actions to take, the effect can be more than just a few seconds here or a few seconds there. If a team trailing at the end of a game has noticed moments when the clock operator has been slow to stop the clock, you can bet that the coach of the trailing team will mention it (and justifiably so). Make your clock operator aware of how important the job is, and stress that he or she take the responsibility seriously.

The NFHS has developed the publication *Instructions for Clock Operators,* available to schools through state association offices and the NFHS. If the clock operator at your game is unaware of this publication, suggest that he or she obtain a copy.

### Line-to-Gain Crew

The members of the line-to-gain crew serve as assistant officials and are partly responsible for promoting smooth operation of the game. Because crew members are serving in an official capacity, they forfeit their rights and privileges as fans and are to refrain from making biased remarks or otherwise showing partiality. If a member of the line-to-gain crew has a reputation of being incompetent or distracting, the referee has the authority to replace that person.

The crew will use a distinctive marker—or clip—to mark the intersection of the yard lines with the chain to maintain its location (see figure 2.9, a and b). The assignment of an additional person to perform this task is recommended. The following are basic procedures and tips

FIGURE 2.9   Officials using (*a*) line-to-gain equipment and (*b*) clip to mark the intersection of the yard lines.

for the line-to-gain crews. In this publication for high school play, references to line-to-gain equipment will be for the traditional two rods and 10-yard chain, unless otherwise indicated.

1. The down-marker operator must remain outside the sideline but within six feet of it. The down-marker operator checks with the linesman following each down to ensure that the proper number is displayed. This person should not change the number of the down or move the marker until instructed to do so by the linesman.

2. The two line-to-gain (chain) operators, positioned on the sideline opposite the press box, should set the chains on the sideline on first down, attach the clip to the chain and then move approximately six feet back from the sideline. Being off the sideline is for the safety of the operators and allows the linesman to move freely along the sideline.

3. When the linesman signals the crew to change positions following a change of possession or a first down, the down marker is placed at the foremost point of the ball first. The crew then places the rear rod in an adjacent position. Whenever an official requests a measurement, the down marker is placed at the spot of the front rod with the previous down indicated.

4. If a ball person is not available, the down-marker operator is responsible for retrieving the ball following a kick try.

5. If a dispute occurs regarding the number of the down, the referee determines the official down number after consulting with the other officials.

6. Following a first down and before the line-to-gain and down markers are moved back from the sideline, officials must fasten a clip on the chain at the back edge of the yard line closest to the rear line-to-gain rod so that they can get an accurate point of reference should a measurement for a first down be required.

7. When the line to gain is the goal line, the line-to-gain crew members remove the equipment from the sideline, and only the down box is used.

8. Whenever play comes near the line-to-gain crew members, they should be ready to drop markers so that players do not run into them.

9. An auxiliary marker or markers (see figure 2.10), which are unofficial line-to-gain ground markers, may be positioned off the

sidelines on both sides of the field. The home-game management decides whether an auxiliary marker will be used, keeping in mind that such use is optional.

10. When used, auxiliary markers should lie flat on the ground and be made of materials that pose no danger to players.

11. An unofficial auxiliary-down indicator may be used on the sideline opposite the official chain and down marker. The person operating this auxiliary marker is considered a member of the line-to-gain crew and has the same restrictions discussed earlier. The line judge will assist in placing the auxiliary marker.

FIGURE 2.10   An auxiliary marker.

12. Use of any replay or television monitoring equipment in making any decision related to the game is prohibited.

The NFHS has developed the publication *Instructions for Line-to-Gain Crews,* available to schools through state association offices and the NFHS.

# Pregame Procedures and Responsibilities

As an official, you need to set a tone of efficiency and professionalism even before the first whistle sounds. Remember that the moment coaches, fans and players see your striped shirt, you are a game authority and must act as one. Although you should not necessarily feel on guard about being scrutinized from the minute you leave your vehicle, you should conduct yourself in a dignified and professional manner on arrival and for the duration of the contest.

Officials should arrive at the game site at least 1 1/2 hours before game time. Tardiness is unacceptable and impairs, perhaps irreparably, credibility and confidence for the rest of the game. As soon as you get to the game site, you should report directly to the game management, introduce yourself and notify them that you are ready to go.

The players participate from whistle to whistle, but officials have duties and procedures to follow not only during play but also before the game, between plays, between quarters and halves, and even after the game. In the rest of this chapter we outline these duties.

## Before the Officials' Conference

After all officials are present, you should meet briefly before performing basic pregame responsibilities, which officials perform even before the pregame officials' conference. Remember that the first interaction you have with coaches before the game may set the tone for subsequent dealings. The following is a rundown of tasks that a five-person crew should perform before the officials' pregame conference. In a four-person crew, the duties of the line judge and back judge are combined.

### Referee

1. Visit each head coach, give coaches a list of officials and notify them of the length of the intermission.
2. Ask each head coach to verify orally, in the presence of the umpire, that all players are legally equipped in compliance with NFHS rules and that coaches and players will exhibit good sportsmanship throughout the game.
3. Check with each head coach for any unusual plays or formations, including any that require prior notification.
4. Secure the name of coaching staff personnel who will be responsible for sideline control of team members and report this information to all officials.
5. Determine if the head coach will be on the sideline so that he can call time-outs.

### Umpire

1. Accompany the referee and examine and rule on any player equipment about which the coach has a question of legality.
2. Review any appropriate documentation for equipment and pads.
3. Obtain and retain documents from medical staff concerning players' conditions or injuries.

## Pregame Officials' Conference

After the officials complete the initial pregame responsibilities, the referee conducts a pregame officials' conference. This meeting should not be confused with the coin toss, which comes later. This conference is only for officials, the clock operator and the line-to-gain crew, who should be in full uniform for the conference. The purpose of the conference is for the participants to familiarize themselves with each other and with various procedures they will follow throughout the game. The meeting should occur approximately one hour before game time. The line judge (in a four-person crew) or back judge (in a five-person crew) will have the correct time, and all officials should synchronize their watches accordingly. The pregame officials' conference should begin with a review of the mechanics of the coin toss and then carry on through scrimmage plays and beyond. To be most effective, the conference should follow a precise outline:

1. Review coverage during scrimmage plays.
   - Running plays, positions and coverage
   - Forward passes, eligibility of receivers and interference
   - Illegal forward passes
   - Numbering requirements checked by the umpire
   - Post-scrimmage kick enforcement procedures
2. Review positions and coverage during scrimmage kicks and free kicks.
   - First touching by the kicking team
   - Fair-catch situations
   - Kicks out of bounds
   - Kick-catching interference
   - Numbering requirements
3. Review general matters.
   - Substitution rule
   - Starting and stopping the clock
   - Procedures during measurement
   - Duties during time-outs and intermission between periods
   - Penalizing personal and unsportsmanlike fouls
   - Penalty administration
   - Overtime procedure, if applicable

- "Momentum" rule as it applies inside the 5-yard line and on scrimmage kicks, free kicks and interceptions of forward passes, fumbles and backward passes
- Positions for goal-line play and try

In addition to this the linesman should check line-to-gain equipment and meet the crew. The line judge should review the starting time and be sure that an auxiliary stopwatch, which records accumulated time, is available. The back judge is responsible for all timing situations, including the 25-second count.

## After the Officials' Conference

After the pregame officials' conference, several pregame duties and procedures remain for officials to carry out. Remember to appear professional at all times and take the game as seriously as the players and coaches do. Keep pregame banter among your crew to a minimum. Keep the following tips in mind.

### All Officials

1. Enter the field together at least 30 minutes before game time.
2. Perform duties in a businesslike manner.
3. Performance and tempo set the tone for the way you will officiate the game.
4. Inspect the playing field and pylons.

### Referee

1. Coordinate the inspection of the playing field and pylons.
2. Direct game management to remove or repair any hazards on or near the field.
3. Approve the clock operator, either scoreboard or sideline.
4. Review signals for starting or stopping the clock with the operator and with the public-address announcer.
5. Inform the coaches of the starting time and where time will be kept.
6. Inform the visiting coach of any change in halftime intermission or if it has been extended (a maximum of five minutes).
7. Keep official score.
8. Instruct the clock operator to time halftime intermission. On your signal, the operator should set the clock at 15 or 20 minutes, start it

when teams have left the field and allow time to elapse completely. Then have the operator immediately reset the clock to three minutes and time warm-ups.

9. Secure and approve the game ball. Use the assigned ball person if two or more balls will be used.

10. Inform the appropriate official to instruct the ball person to hold the ball not in use and move up and down the sideline or sidelines. The ball person should not enter the playing field. When the ball is dead following a change of possession, the ball person hands it to the nearest official. The ball person should not hand a new ball until instructed.

### Umpire

1. Check player equipment when requested by a head coach.

2. Know that you are the final authority on legality of equipment.

3. Do not permit use of any illegal equipment.

### Linesman

1. Secure and check the line-to-gain equipment, down marker and all auxiliary equipment. Ensure that the chain is marked at the halfway point with tape.

2. Check to see that home management has distinctive vests or jackets for the crew.

3. Remind the crew of their duties and responsibilities.

4. Instruct the line-to-gain crew that you will use your heel to mark at the sideline where they should place the rear rod for every first down.

5. Work on the side where the line-to-gain equipment is located, which is opposite the press box, if there is one.

6. Ask home management to specify a side if there is no press box.

### Line Judge

1. Carry an accurate watch that has the correct time (when in a four-person crew).

2. Other officials synchronize their watches with yours.

3. Check the starting time and assist in getting the game started promptly.

4. When there is no field clock, time the game (in a four-person crew).

5. Take care of the game ball after the referee has approved it.

### Back Judge

1. Secure the correct time and carry an accurate watch.
2. Assist with securing the sidelines.
3. When there is no field clock, time the game.
4. Be responsible for 25-second clock, if used.

# Coin Toss

The coin toss can be held off the field if both coaches agree, but most fans enjoy the drama of the midfield toss. This issue should not be a primary concern of the officials, of course, but midfield tosses are preferable unless circumstances make them awkward, such as band performances or pre-game ceremonies not related to the game. Coin-toss procedures follow.

### Referee

As the referee, you are the lead official, and fulfilling that duty begins even before the game does. A calm, friendly, professional, yet authoritarian, attitude lets everyone know that you are in charge. The coin toss is as good a place as any to let that attitude come to the fore. You lead the proceedings and set the tone for interaction during the game.

#### Pregame Toss

1. If the coin toss occurs off the field, simulate the results at the center of the field three minutes before the start of game or as directed by the state association.
2. About five minutes (or as directed by the state association) before game time, escort to the center of the field the captain or captains of the team whose team box is on the side opposite the line-to-gain equipment. The actual toss should be at the three-minute mark for both four- and five-person crews (see figure 2.11, a and b).
3. Have captains face each other with their backs to the sidelines.
4. After the umpire introduces the captain or captains, introduce the captains to each other and give them instructions.
5. In the presence of the umpire, instruct the visiting captain to choose heads or tails before the toss. Inform the captains that if you don't catch the coin, you will repeat the toss. After making the toss and determining the winner, place a hand on the winning captain's shoulder and have him choose one of following options:
   a. Kick or receive
   b. Defend a goal
   c. Defer the choice to the second half

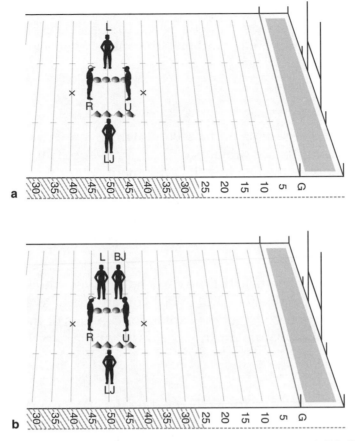

FIGURE 2.11   Coin-toss positions for (*a*) four-person and (*b*) five-person crews.

6. If the winner chooses not to defer and makes a choice, give the opposing captain choice of the remaining options.

7. If the winner of the toss defers, step toward the press box and give the penalty-declined signal. Give the opposing captain choice of the options and then give the deferring captain choice of the remaining options.

8. Place captains in position facing each other with their backs toward the goal their teams will defend.

9. While facing in the same direction as the captain who chose first, signal his choice in this manner:

   a. Swing your leg, simulating a kick.

   b. Make a catching motion, simulating receiving.

c. If the captain choosing first elected to defend a goal, point with both arms extended toward that goal line. Then move to the other captain and give the appropriate signal for his choice.

10. Dismiss captains.

### Second-Half Choices

1. Before the beginning of the second half, escort to the center of the field the captain or captains of the team whose team box is on the side opposite the line-to-gain equipment.

2. Obtain second-half choices and give the appropriate signal or signals to the press box.

3. Dismiss captains after giving any further instructions.

## Umpire

You should get to the field a little early so that you know which team is on which side of the field. That way, you are ready to act with more certainty when you go to get the captain or captains of the team that is your responsibility. Banter during the toss is unnecessary. Let the referee take charge.

### Pregame Toss

1. About five minutes (or as directed by the state association) before game time, escort to the center of field the captain or captains of the team whose team box is on the side where the line-to-gain equipment is located.

2. After introducing the captains to the referee, remain with the referee to listen to the instructions and record the toss options.

### Second-Half Choices

1. On the signal from the referee, escort the captain or captains to the center of the field. Again, knowing which team is your responsibility is important. By this time, you should know who the team captains are.

2. Remain with the referee and captains and check on the options given to the teams to ensure accuracy. You should listen so that the referee is not the only official aware of the options. You never know when you might be called on.

## Linesman and Judges

Now is the time for the linesman and judges to establish that they supervise the line-to-gain crew, the hands-on workers of the chain. The officials need not be bullies, but a firm attitude helps, particularly because members of the line-to-gain crew often are home-team fans or parents.

**Pregame Toss**

1. The linesman gives instruction to the line-to-gain crew.
2. The linesman (in a four-person crew) or back judge (in a five-person crew), whose team box is on the side where the line-to-gain equipment is located, remains at the inbounds mark to keep team members who are not involved in the toss between himself and the sideline.
3. The linesman obtains the football of the kicking team's choice from the line judge. A simple toss or handing of the ball will do. No one cares if you have great hands or if the line judge has a great arm.
4. The line judge, whose team box is on the side opposite the line-to-gain equipment, remains at the inbounds mark to keep team members who are not involved in the toss between himself and the sideline.
5. The back judge observes the team on the linesman's side while the linesman completes instructions to the line-to-gain crew.

**Second-Half Choices**

1. The linesman (in a four-person crew) or back judge (in a five-person crew) on the sideline with the line-to-gain crew
   a. reviews procedures and corrects problems with the line-to-gain crew,
   b. indicates the end of the field where the line-to-gain crew will be before the kickoff and
   c. assumes the same position at the inbounds mark that he did before the first-half kickoff.
2. The line judge on the sideline opposite the line-to-gain crew
   a. assumes the same position at the inbounds mark that he did before the first-half kickoff and
   b. obtains the football of the kicking team's choice and gives it to the linesman.
3. The back judge observes the team on the linesman's side while the linesman gives instructions to the line-to-gain crew.

### *All Officials*

Officials will naturally be anxious for the game to begin, even a little nervous. But do your best to keep your emotions in check. Be calm, authoritative and professional. Setting the tone for the game begins during the initial interaction among coaches, players and officials. Realize that although coaches and players have other things on their minds, they are observing your actions.

### Pregame Toss

1. At the conclusion of the toss procedures and after the captains have been dismissed, move together for final instructions from the referee.

2. Record which team has first choice for the second half.

3. At the referee's signal, hustle to kickoff positions. The linesman and the judge or judges clear the sidelines before going to kickoff position.

### Second-Half Choices

1. After choices are completed, come together at the center of the field for any final instructions.

2. Hustle to kickoff positions. The linesman and the judge or judges clear the sidelines before going to kickoff position.

# Additional Responsibilities

Besides performing the normal activities outlined earlier, you should be aware of other responsibilities and duties. The whistle, the clock, player safety and other details are important to keeping the game moving and keeping it safe. You will not have these responsibilities on every play, but you should avoid being surprised by any possible situation.

## Sounding the Whistle

Sounding the whistle may seem like a simple procedure, but a technique is involved. Sounding the whistle definitively and in a timely fashion is extremely important to the flow of the game, the safety of the players and the participants' perception of the official's authority. All officials should observe the following guidelines:

- Player safety is your first responsibility.
- Find the ball before sounding the whistle.
- To prevent an early whistle, be sure that you see the ball in possession of the runner who is down or a stoppage of forward progress.
- When sounding the whistle, do it quickly and loudly.
- If you're in position and alert, you should be able to keep the ball in view.
- Be ready to assist the covering official after the whistle has sounded.
- Use a beanbag to mark the spot of the end of the run if the whistle is sounded inadvertently.

If you're the official covering the runner, make certain that you first find the ball before sounding your whistle. When the call becomes dead, sound your whistle quickly and loudly. Then move in quickly to be certain that all action stops on the whistle. If you sound the whistle inadvertently, the ball becomes dead immediately. The location and status of the ball will determine the location at which the ball will be put in play and the down number of the next down.

## The Clock

Officials rely heavily on a competent clock operator, but our focus here is the officials' responsibility in making sure that the clock is stopped and restarted at the proper times. Knowledge of when the clock should be stopped and restarted is paramount to a fair contest, and making a definitive start- or stop-clock signal (see figure 2.12, a-d, and figure 2.13, a and b, on page 37) to the clock operator is just as important. The clock

*(continued)*

FIGURE 2.12   *(a-d)* Official signaling start clock.

FIGURE 2.12   (*continued*)

stops during a football game for several reasons. An official should stop the clock (by giving the proper signal twice) in these situations:

- The down ends following a foul.
- An official's time-out is taken.
- A charged time-out or TV or radio time-out is granted.
- The period ends.
- The ball is out of bounds.
- A forward pass is incomplete.
- A score or touchback occurs.
- A fair catch is made or awarded.
- An obvious first down occurs.

Additionally, an official's time-out requires that the clock be stopped when the ball becomes dead in these situations:

FIGURE 2.13 (*a and b*) Official signaling stop clock.

- For measurement of a possible first down
- Before the first down is declared
- Following a change of team possession
- When captains and coaches are required to be notified of time remaining
- For a player who appears to be injured
- For a player in need of equipment repair
- To dry or change the ball
- For unusual heat or humidity that may create a health risk to players
- When a coach-referee conference concerning misapplication of a rule results in the referee's altering a ruling
- After a foul to administer the penalty
- For unusual delays in getting the ball ready for play
- A TV or radio time-out

- The one minute between periods and following a try, successful field goal or safety

Aside from the reasons previously mentioned, there are also a few other reasons to stop the clock. These are:

- As provided by rule
- If a team attempts to consume time
- If the covering official determines that the ball reaches the line to gain

Please note that if the signal to stop the clock is erroneously given, restart it immediately on discovering the error.

Another set of procedures governs starting the clock. The referee gives the start-clock signal using two turns of an arm. The referee and the clock operator must communicate effectively. They discuss how they will communicate before the game begins. Ineffective communication can result in too much or too little time being on the clock. Either circumstance can have a direct effect on the outcome of the game.

Start the clock on the ready-for-play-signal if the clock was stopped in these situations:

- For an official's time-out other than a new series for the defensive team or a new series following a legal kick
- For a dead ball after a foul if there was no charged time-out during the dead-ball interval, if the down is not an extension of a period or try, if there was no abuse of the timing rule or a delay-of-game penalty, or if the action that caused the down to end did not also cause the clock to stop
- Because of an inadvertent whistle

You will also start the clock on the snap if the clock stopped for any reason other than those listed in the previous section. If the clock starts on the snap, the official gives no visible signal to start the clock. In addition to this, start the clock on a free kick when the ball is touched other than the first touching by the kicking team. Legal touching of the free kick can be by either team. The covering official signals the clock to start by using two turns of the arm.

Of course, there are also clock-winding procedures. Keep the clock winding and give the signal if the ball becomes dead inbounds near the sideline. The official should use normal coverage. After determining that the ball is dead, give the start-clock signal using only two turns of the arm.

If the ball becomes dead near a sideline and a first down is gained, the covering official should use normal coverage. After determining that the ball is dead, give the start-clock signal using only two turns of the arm and then the time-out signal.

## Shortening Periods

Rarely will you have to shorten periods, but you should know the procedure. Lightning or other weather events are common reasons for shortening a period. No one wants to shorten a period or a game, but safety comes first—for players, coaches, officials and fans. The procedures in this case are simple. The referee confers with the opposing coaches to finalize the decision and receive any instructions. He then indicates the end of the shortened period by giving the proper signal.

## Penalty Marker and Beanbag

Tossing a penalty flag might seem like a simple task, but like everything an official does, using the proper method is important. You have no need to showboat by tossing a flag 25 yards down the field. At the same time, you should toss the marker so that it is obvious that a penalty has occurred. Discretion, common sense and credibility are the key concepts here.

You should keep your penalty marker tucked out of sight. When you see an infraction, you'll use your marker to mark the yard line where the infraction occurred. Your discretion, position and the game situation determine whether you drop or toss the penalty marker (see figures 2.14 and 2.15, a-c, on pages 40 and 41).

Correct use of the beanbag is important as well. Rarely does anyone other than the officials even notice the beanbag, but dropping it in appropriate spots is important (see figure 2.16, a and b, on page 41). When use of the beanbag is called for, simply drop it on the appropriate yard line. Keep in mind that the beanbag is to serve as an aid to enforcement and not an absolute reference point.

## Declaring the Ball Ready for Play

Declaring the ball ready for play is an every-play activity that takes synchronization between officials to keep play flowing smoothly. If you are not in tune with other members on your crew and confusion occurs

FIGURE 2.14    (*a-c*) Official properly dropping flag.

in getting the ball in play, both game flow and your credibility suffer. Smoothness and awareness are important on every play.

Although all officials must hustle to their proper positions and work as a team to prevent delay, the referee is primarily responsible for declaring the ball ready for play. After the ball is spotted, he checks that the other officials are in position and ready. Then he announces the down, using his fingers or his fist for fourth down, sounds the whistle, gives the ready-for-play signal (see figure 2.17, a and b, on page 42) to start the 25-second count and moves to position while keeping his eye on the ball. If necessary, he starts the clock. A maximum of three seconds are required to spot and mark. If a quick snap is imminent, the referee should get in position to observe the snap before giving the ready-for-play signal. In this case, the umpire stands over the ball until the referee signals him to move.

FIGURE 2.15 (*a-c*) Official properly tossing flag.

FIGURE 2.16 (*a and b*) Official properly dropping beanbag.

FIGURE 2.17    (*a and b*) Official signaling ready for play.

## After a Try or Field Goal and Before a Free Kick

The moments after a score can be chaotic for players and coaches, but you must refrain from being caught up in the hoopla. Your actions and body language should not be different after a score than they are at any other time of the game. Keep the game flowing and enforce the time restrictions to prevent anything from getting out of hand. The following section explains the duties of each official in this situation.

### Referee

1. In a four-person crew, start the 60-second interval before the ensuing kickoff as players and officials move out to their kickoff positions. The linesman should have the ball. In a five-person crew, the back judge will time this interval and notify you, the referee.

2. At 45 seconds, if teams are not in position to play, signal the umpire, linesman and line judge by pointing directly at them to give their teams a 15-second warning.

3. Count players.

4. Pick up ready signs from the crew when they are in free-kick positions.

5. At the end of the 60-second interval, promptly give the ready-for-play signal with a sharp blast of the whistle.

6. Penalize for delay of game if the ball is not kicked within 25 seconds after giving the ready-for-play signal.

## Umpire

1. Move up your own sideline to prevent illegal conferences and clear the sidelines.

2. Be alert for a signal from the referee (pointing directly toward you) to give your team a 15-second warning; go to the team huddle and say, "Coach, the ball will be marked ready for play in 15 seconds."

3. Count the receiving team's players.

4. Be sure that the sideline is clear before you give the ready sign to the referee.

## Linesman

1. Obtain the ball (four-person crew). Move up your own sideline to clear it for play.

2. Check the line-to-gain crew for questions and positions.

3. Be alert for a signal from the referee (pointing directly toward you) to give your team (not the umpire's team) a 15-second warning; go to the team huddle and say, "Coach, the ball will be marked ready for play in 15 seconds."

4. Proceed to the hash mark.

5. While at the hash mark, count the kicking team's players, point out the referee to the kicker, and instruct the kicker to wait for the referee to give the ready-for-play signal before kicking.

6. If the kicker will not accept the ball, place the ball at the free-kick spot and assume your final position by moving to the sideline at the same time the line judge moves.

7. Be sure that the sideline is clear before giving the ready sign to the referee.

## Line Judge (in Four- and Five-Person Crews)

1. Move up your own sideline to clear it for play.

2. Be alert for a signal from the referee (pointing directly toward you) to give your team a 15-second warning; go to the team huddle and say, "Coach, the ball will be marked ready for play in 15 seconds."

3. Proceed to the hash mark.

4. While at the hash mark, count the receiving team's players and identify the free-kick line for the receiving team.

5. Assume your final position by moving to the sideline at the same time the linesman moves.

6. Be sure that the sideline is clear before giving the ready sign to the referee.

### Back Judge (Five-Person Crew)

1. Start the 60-second count for the ensuing kickoff as players and officials move out to their positions. The linesman should have the ball.

2. If teams are not in position to play at the 45-second mark, notify the referee, who in turn will signal the linesman and line judge to give 15-second warnings to their teams.

3. Obtain the ball. Move to the same sideline as the line-to-gain equipment.

4. Count the kicking team's players.

5. Assist the linesman in clearing the sideline before giving the ready sign to the referee.

### All Officials

1. Observe the action.

2. Prevent unnecessary delays.

3. Encourage both teams to take free-kick positions quickly.

4. Hustle to the free-kick position.

## Correcting Timing Errors

You need to follow two important guidelines concerning timing errors. First, correct timing errors only if the mistakes are readily evident and have resulted in an acknowledged discrepancy. Second, errors of judgment are not open for correction. The error must be mechanical or result from human failure to administer a timing rule correctly.

Officials and timekeepers make mistakes. When timing mistakes occur, you must correct them quickly and decisively. Nothing damages credibility more than failure to do anything about a timing mistake obvious to everyone in the stadium. When you know a mistake has been made, fix it. Depending on your role, you should do the following in the case of a timing error.

### Referee

1. You are authorized to correct an obvious error in timing if it is discovered before the second live ball following the error, unless the period has officially ended.

2. You must be able to determine within reasonable limits the interval of time involved when putting time on or taking time off the clock. You may consult the operator.

### All Officials

1. Note time on the clock during dead-ball intervals especially when the clock is stopped.
2. Monitor time closely if problems arise with the operation of the clock.
3. Assist the referee as much as possible.

## Coach-Referee Conference

You should strive to balance a coach's right to comment and ask questions with your obligation to keep the game moving. Do not become argumentative. Stay calm when explaining your actions or interpretations. A coach can disagree but should maintain decorum. Your job is to strike the proper balance. The purposes of a coach-referee conference are to allow a review of possible misapplication or mis-interpretation of rules by officials and to allow for correction when an error has been made. Following are the correct procedures for coach-referee conferences:

1. A coach must request a conference before the ball becomes live following the play that is to be reviewed, unless the period has officially ended.
2. The coach may call a time-out or direct a player to request a time-out to confer with the referee regarding possible misapplication of a rule.
3. If an official grants a time-out, it is charged to the requesting team.
4. The referee (accompanied by the linesman or line judge) and coach confer at the sideline directly in front of the team box in the field of play.
5. If the referee determines that the rule has been applied correctly, the time-out remains charged to the team. If the team has used all permissible time-outs, the referee throws his penalty flag and calls a foul for delay of game.
6. If the referee determines that the rule has been applied incorrectly, the correction is made immediately and the time-out previously charged to the team becomes an official's time-out. The referee will review and explain the situation to the opposing coach before continuing the game.

## Coach Disqualification Procedure

As with the coach-official conference, you must avoid becoming emotional. If a coach steps over the line, you must disqualify him. Follow the procedures relevant to your role. Remember, you should judge this circumstance as just another interpretation of a rule. Above all, keep your cool.

The referee (accompanied by the linesman or line judge) must provide the coach with the reason for disqualification and require the coach to vacate the stadium area. If the coach does not leave, inform him that noncompliance could lead to forfeiture. Locate the local administration for assistance. Do not continue the contest until the coach vacates the stadium area. If necessary, you may forfeit the contest. You must comply with all state association reporting requirements.

The linesman or line judge should accompany the referee to the sideline and assist if necessary. The linesman or line judge should also observe all players and notify the opposing coach of disqualification.

The referee or calling official must notify the coach of all unsporting fouls against him that carry a 15-yard penalty, such as improper conduct toward an official, failure of a player to wear required equipment or having more than three coaches in the 2-yard area between the sideline and team-box area. Any coach who receives two unsportsmanlike conduct fouls (see figure 2.18) must vacate the stadium area, without exception. If the first foul is severe enough, officials can disqualify the coach without the occurrence of a second foul.

## Controlling the Sideline and Team Box

During competition, emotions sometimes run high. Keeping coaches and players in their assigned positions on the sidelines helps prevent problems. Nothing is more chaotic (and dangerous) than having players and coaches creep onto the field; therefore a sideline warning is given when nonplayers are outside the team box, but not on the field or when coaches violate the coaching box rule (a maximum of three coaches may be in the coaches' area).

Constant vigilance by officials is necessary. Because participants quickly forget reminders when big plays or situations arise, make sure that coaches know you are serious about maintaining order. As an official, you must consistently administer and enforce team-box and coaching-box restrictions. Be firm and professional in enforcing that restriction so that all officials have enough room to work. The action taken on each occurrence of these offenses is as follows:

FIGURE 2.18  Official signaling unsportsmanlike conduct.

- First offense: No penalty is issued and the official should give a sideline warning signal (see figure 2.19).
- Second offense: A 5-yard penalty is issued and the official should give dead-ball and sideline interference signals.
- Third offense: A 15-yard penalty is issued and the official should give dead-ball, sideline interference and noncontact foul signals .

You should note that a warning and 5-yard penalty for sideline interference do not count as fouls leading to ejection.

### First Violation
The detailed procedure for officials when issuing only a sideline warning on the first violation is as follows:

1. The covering official sounds a whistle and reports the infraction to the referee. The referee gives the proper signal and indicates the offending sideline.

FIGURE 2.19   Official giving a sideline warning signal to indicate the first offense of the team and coaching-box restrictions.

2. The covering official informs the coach of the warning. The communication should include a reminder that further violations will result in distance penalties.
3. All officials record the time of the sideline warning.

### Second Violation
The detailed procedure for officials when issuing dead-ball and sideline interference signals on the second violation is as follows:
1. The covering official drops a penalty marker, sounds the whistle and reports the infraction to the referee.
2. The referee gives approved signals, and the umpire assesses the distance penalty.
3. The covering official orally informs the coach and reminds him that each subsequent offense will result in a 15-yard penalty.
4. All officials record the time and period in which the penalty is assessed.

### Third and Subsequent Violations
The detailed procedure for officials when issuing dead-ball, sideline interference and noncontact foul signals on the third and subsequent violations is as follows:

1. The covering official drops a penalty marker, sounds the whistle and reports the infraction to the referee.
2. The referee gives approved signals, and the umpire assesses the distance penalty.
3. The covering official orally informs the coach and reminds him that each subsequent offense will result in a 15-yard penalty.
4. All officials record the time and period in which the penalty is assessed.

## Controlling Team Personnel Altercations

Altercations among athletes can be stressful and potentially danger-ous situations if not properly handled. Sometimes, fights between highly charged athletes are unavoidable. But dealing with altercations quickly and with authority goes a long way toward keeping them from escalating.

If the altercation is in your area you should attempt to stop the initial confrontation. That recommendation doesn't mean becoming involved in the altercation. Grabbing a player by the jersey or face mask is unnecessary and might escalate the situation. But a declarative, forceful presence, achieved perhaps by stepping between the two players, could stop the situation from going further. Also remember to keep the whistle out of your mouth. If you are unable to stop the altercation, step back and record the uniform number of each player and team personnel involved. If you are the linesman or line judge, you should alert the coach on your side to keep all team personnel off the playing area.

# Postgame Procedures and Responsibilities

When the whistle sounds to end the fourth quarter, your job is not fin-ished. You must make sure that things are still running smoothly, par-ticularly if the game has been emotional or confrontational.

At the end of a regulation game, the referee indicates the end of fourth period using the proper signal. All officials immediately leave the field together, neither avoiding nor seeking out coaches. Officials should neither discuss the game on the field nor make any public statement about the game to news media. Officials should also report any flagrant irregularity or disqualification to the state association office when appli-cable. If your state association has additional penalties for fighting, follow the reporting procedure.

In an overtime situation, players and coaches will be especially tense. You must remain calm and follow proper overtime procedures:

1. Hold the coin toss at the center of the field, using general coin-toss mechanics.
2. The toss winner shall choose to be on offense or defense or choose the end of field where the ball will be put in play.
3. To start each new series, the team may designate the location of the ball between inbounds lines.
4. The referee indicates the winner of the toss by placing a hand on the winner's shoulder:
   a. Position the offensive captain facing the goal toward which the ball will be advanced and place the defensive captain facing his opponent and the opposite goal.
   b. Give the first-down signal toward the goal being used.

## Staying Current

If you want to know the rules and positioning thoroughly as they apply to both four- and five-person crews, hence enhancing your ability to make quick decisions that will inspire confidence, you should study regularly.

Besides this book, the NFHS has developed a number of supplementary materials that can help officials develop competency in the rules of football. These include the *NFHS Football Case Book, NFHS Football Handbook, NFHS Football Simplified and Illustrated* and *NFHS Football Preseason Guides*, as well as a series of audiovisual materials. Those responsible for training officials use Parts I and II of the Football Rules Examination and the Official's Mechanics Examination. State high school associations generally conduct a series of rules interpretation meetings, at which attendance is required for those officials who are eligible to work games in that state.

Visiting the NFHS Web site (www.NFHS.org) and high school state association Web sites can also be helpful in keeping you current. The NFHS Web site contains information about educational possibilities for officials, equipment, sports medicine, publications, officials' chat rooms and other useful data. The role of the NFHS and state high school associations is to support and assist members in becoming more proficient. That purpose also applies to officials. Staying informed about various NFHS and high school association forums, functions and publications can help you carry out a complex assignment.

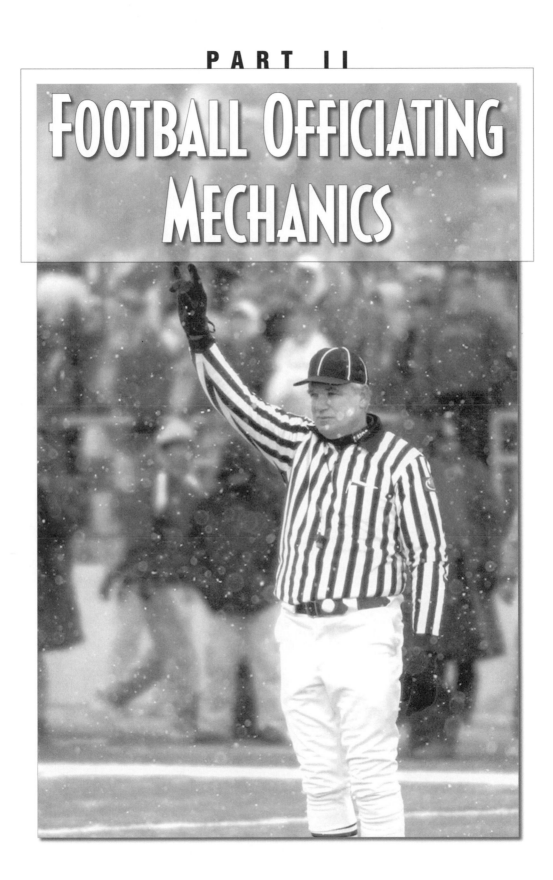

# PART II

# FOOTBALL OFFICIATING MECHANICS

# FOUR-PERSON CREW MECHANICS

Chapters 3 and 4 make up the core of *Officiating Football*. The following two chapters deal with the every-play activity of all officials, for both four- and five-person crews. In these chapters we deal with positioning before plays, reading the proper keys and reacting correctly—from kickoff through plays from scrimmage to end-of-game activities.

You should acquire a thorough understanding of all officials' responsibilities on every play and in every situation. Digesting that much information is a formidable task, but you can achieve it through study and experience. As your understanding of situations and responsibilities increases, your reactions will become second nature.

To begin, review the starting positions of each official on plays from scrimmage when operating in a four-person crew, illustrated in figure 3.1.

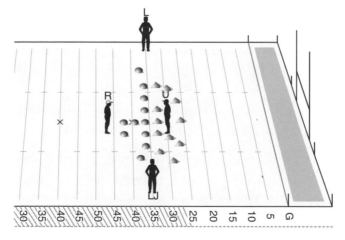

FIGURE 3.1  Starting positions on standard plays from scrimmage.

- *Referee.* On the passing-arm side of the quarterback, approximately 10 to 12 yards deep and at least as wide as the tight end. The referee must be able to view the backs and the tackle on the far side of the field.
- *Umpire.* Three to 8 yards behind the defensive line and between the defensive ends, keeping the snap in full view. The umpire must not interfere with the vision or movement of defensive backs. He should vary his position so that players cannot use him as interference.
- *Linesman and line judge* (on opposite sides of the field). Straddling the line of scrimmage not closer than 9 yards outside the widest offensive player.

# Kickoff

The kickoff requires officials to cover more territory than they do on any other play in football. Covering the whole field on a kickoff requires each official to handle specific responsibilities (see figure 3.2). If each official covers the ground to which he is assigned and reacts properly to situations, the large area of coverage isn't a problem.

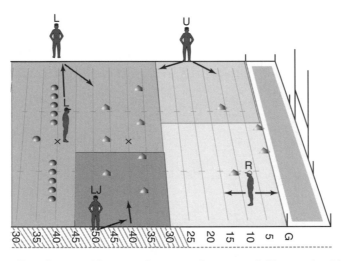

FIGURE 3.2   Starting positions and areas of responsibility on the kickoff.

Each official has different prekick responsibilities and duties for onside kicks (see figure 3.3). Each official covers different zones of the field. Individual officials must stick to their areas of responsibility to achieve full-field coverage. Following is a summary of duties for all officials and for each official in the crew.

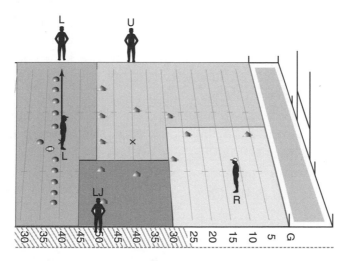

FIGURE 3.3 Starting positions for an obvious onside kick situation.

### All Officials

The covering official or officials signal the clock to start when the kick is touched other than the first touching by the kicker. The first touching can occur only in the 10-yard belt between the two free-kick lines. For a kick out of bounds between the goal lines, sound the whistle, give the time-out signal and mark the spot with a beanbag. Then determine if the receiving team touched the ball inbounds and toss a flag if the receiving team did not touch the ball.

Always maintain position to cover the sideline. When the ball becomes dead in this area, sound the whistle and give the time-out signal. Carry the beanbag in your hands so that you're ready to drop it as soon as it becomes necessary.

### Referee

Before the kick, your position as the referee is near the receiving team's 5- or 10-yard line and inside the sideline opposite the linesman. Count the receiving team's players and check the positions of other officials. Then hold an arm above your head to request the ready sign from other officials and the kicker. After you have received all ready signs, drop your arm and sound your whistle to signal the kicker to kick the ball.

- *Short free kick.* If you expect a short free kick, take a position near the receiving team's 10-yard line and be ready to assist the other officials.
- *Kick down the middle.* Signal the clock to start when the kick is touched other than the first touching by the kicking team. Then pick up the runner and follow him until releasing him to the covering official.

- *Deep kick.* Retreat to the goal line to rule on a touchback. If the kick is caught inside the 5-yard line and the player is downed in the end zone or if the ball goes out of bounds there, mark the spot of the catch with your beanbag and rule on whether the player's momentum took him into the end zone.

- *Kick outside the opposite inbounds lines.* Move cautiously with the play. Observe the action of players near the runner and serve as the cleanup behind, to the side of and around the runner.

- *Kick out of bounds.* Determine if the receiving team touched or last touched the ball inbounds.

### Umpire

Before the kick, your position as the umpire is at the receiving team's 20-yard line on the sideline opposite the line judge. You must monitor the bench area and then move to the sideline opposite the line judge. Be certain that coaches, players, substitutes and other people are in proper location. Count the players on the receiving team. When you complete the count, hold an arm above your head to indicate that you are ready for the kick to be made.

- *After the kickoff.* Maintain your position, covering your sideline at all times. Also observe the legality of blocks and action away from the ball when you are not covering the runner.

- *Short free kick.* If you expect a short free kick, position yourself near the receiving team's 40-yard line. Be alert for the first touching by the kicking team or for a kick that does not cross the receiving team's free-kick line.

- *Kick to your side.* Signal the clock to start when the kick is touched, other than the first touching by the kicking team. Then pick up the runner and follow him. When the ball becomes dead, sound your whistle and give the time-out signal. Be alert for the first touching by the kicking team and mark the spot with your beanbag. Mark the spot where the kick goes out of bounds on your side of the field. If the receiving team touches the ball inbounds, mark the spot with your beanbag. If the receiving team does not touch the ball inbounds, drop the penalty marker.

- *Kick to the opposite side of the field.* Move cautiously toward the play and observe the action of players near the runner.

### Linesman

Before the kick, you must take charge of the ball. Your position is at the kicking team's free-kick line in the side zone so that you can monitor the bench area and assist the kicking team in getting into position. Move onto the field to the kicker. After checking the legality of the kicking tee, hand the kicker the ball, point out the referee and instruct the kicker to wait for the referee's signal before kicking. If the kicker is not ready, place the ball on the ground and then proceed to the sideline. Count the kicking team's players and move to your position just outside the sideline on the kicking team's free-kick line on the side where the line-to-gain equipment is located. Be certain that coaches, players, substitutes and other individuals are in proper locations, and then hold your arm above your head to indicate that you are ready.

Watch for any infractions involving the kicking team's free-kick line. If a dead-ball foul occurs, administer the penalty and place the ball ready.

After the kick, be alert for the first touching by the kicking team. Mark the spot with your beanbag. You should also be alert for a kick that does not cross the receiving team's free-kick line.

If a penalty for a foul occurs before the kick ends and a rekick is necessary, enforce the penalty and repeat the procedure explained previously. Mark the out-of-bounds spot if the kick goes out of bounds in your area either by dropping your beanbag on the spot if touched inbounds by the receiving team or by dropping the penalty marker if not touched inbounds by the receiving team. Watch initial blocks by players near the receiving team's free-kick line and the action against the kicker and holder. Cover to the receiver's 45-yard line. After the ball has gone downfield, move deliberately in that direction while watching for fouls away from the ball. Maintain your position, covering the sideline at all times. Be in position to take over coverage of a runner moving into your area on a long return.

### *Line Judge*

Before the kick, be certain that coaches, players, substitutes and other individuals are in proper locations. Your position is at the receiving team's free-kick line, outside the sideline and opposite the linesman. Count the kicking team's players, identify the free-kick line and hold an arm above your head to indicate that you are ready. You should also watch for any infractions involving the receiving team's free-kick line.

If you expect a short free kick, take your position on the receiving team's free-kick line and be alert for the first touching by the kicking team or for a kick that does not cross the receiving team's free-kick line.

After the kick, be alert for the first touching by the kicking team. Mark the spot of the first touching with your beanbag. You should also watch initial blocks in your area. If the ball becomes dead in your area, including before crossing the receiving team's free-kick line, sound your whistle, give the time-out signal and mark the spot where the kick goes out of bounds on your side of field with the penalty marker if not touched inbounds by the receiving team. After the ball has gone downfield, move deliberately in that direction while watching for fouls away from the ball. Cover 15 yards down the sideline.

Although the play occurs infrequently, a shrewd coach may try to pull off a field-goal attempt by a free kick after a fair catch or awarded fair catch. This situation presents a perfect example of the importance of knowing your duties, regardless of the situation. All you need to know is that the referee determines whether the kick is successful. He takes a position behind and directly between the uprights. All other officials follow the mechanics they use for a kickoff.

# Plays From Scrimmage

You will spend most of your time during a game monitoring plays from scrimmage—running plays, passing plays, field-goal attempts from various parts of the field, punts and goal-line situations. Because this action makes up the bulk of the game, you should know what you're doing in these situations without having to think twice. Reflex reactions result in fluid games. The essential rhythm of a football game can only be achieved if the choreographers, that is, the officials, stay in step.

## Reading Keys

As an official, your duties begin before the snap. By considering contextual cues and reading keys, you can anticipate plays and make the necessary reactions. For instance, a defensive back or linebacker approaching the line before the snap is a good cue that a blitz is possible. If a lineman's first move is forward, you know that the offense is executing a running play. If a quarterback is in the shotgun formation and there is no back in the backfield, watch for a pass. These are just a few examples of hints that help you anticipate the action, which in turn helps you be in the proper position.

Similarly, being aware of keys (specific players that officials watch at the start of a play) will help you anticipate plays. You will still have to make adjustments after you read keys, but knowing tendencies and player positions will help you make the adjustments more quickly. Keys do not necessarily determine coverage for the entire play. You must be prepared to react to the play as it develops.

In four-person coverage, the keys are straightforward—each wing official is responsible for action by the players entering his zone. The key for each of these officials would be the action of the first player into that zone.

In discussing and illustrating keys, several definitions are useful:

- *Strength of formation.* Determined by the number of eligible receivers on a particular side of the offensive formation. This designation depends not on the number of linemen on each side of the center but rather on the number of eligible receivers outside the tackles. If there is no strong side, strength is declared to the line judge's side.
- *Tight end.* The end man on the line of scrimmage lined up no more than 4 yards from the nearest offensive lineman.
- *Back in backfield.* A player in the backfield between the tackles at the snap. Whether a team lines up in a double wing T, I-formation, one-back pro formation or any other formation, the position of the backs in the backfield can sometimes affect keys and indicate to an official what kind of play is coming.
- *Trips.* Three or more receivers outside one of the offensive tackles. In this formation, common plays include deep and intermediate passes. Pass blocking is prevalent.
- *Player in motion.* A player running behind and parallel to the line of scrimmage before the ball is snapped.

## Running Plays

In high school football, most teams run from scrimmage far more than they pass. Some teams pass often, of course, but the point is this: Reacting to running plays will be a large part of your responsibility when teams are lined up to run a play from scrimmage (see figure 3.4). The area of responsibility is often smaller on running plays than it is on passing or

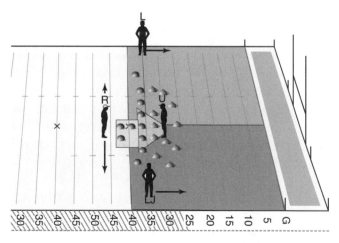

FIGURE 3.4   Starting positions and areas of responsibility on running and passing plays.

kicking plays, but because you will spend much of your time officiating running plays, you should not judge the importance of your duties by the actual yardage you are responsible for.

Physical, tight, close-quarters action is often the norm on running plays. That kind of action is sometimes difficult to observe, but your scrutiny is required to ensure fair play and safety. Knowing the following officials' responsibilities on running plays can enhance both safe play and fairness.

### Referee

After the ball is spotted, declare the ball ready for play by using established procedure. Take a position behind the offense (the distance back or to the side varies with the formation of the offense but is usually 3 to 4 yards deeper than deepest back) on the passing-arm side of the quarterback. You should be able to view the tackle on the far side and the backs. At this point, you check

- the 25-second count,
- the 1-second count after a huddle or shift,
- the number of offensive players and eligible backs,
- snap irregularities and movement of linemen, and
- illegal shifts or players in motion.

You will then give the signal for 11 players to the linesman and line judge. After the snap, you are responsible for keying the tackle on the opposite side. If he blocks aggressively, read the run. If he pass blocks, read the pass. You also read the ball, runner and action around him to the neutral zone.

If the action is not in the direction of your original position, move toward or parallel to the scrimmage line, maintaining position approximately in line with the runner's progress. You should delay moving immediately toward the line of scrimmage to avoid hindering a reverse or delayed play and to assure maximum vision of the play. If the play results in a score and no foul occurs, give the touchdown signal and record the score. Move behind the play toward the side of the field to which the play advances to cover the runner if he is downed near the neutral zone. You should check

- illegal use of hands by offensive players and action behind the ball and away from the runner near the neutral zone,
- action on the quarterback after a handoff,
- the signal from the linesman or line judge indicating the foremost point of the ball on quick line plays,

- a backward or forward pass when the ball is thrown and
- the out-of-bounds spot behind the neutral zone.

You should continue to observe action behind the neutral zone before leaving the area. You are responsible for the runner until he crosses the neutral zone.

When the ball is dead, you should move quickly to its location, be certain of ball location before sounding the whistle and signal the number of the next down. You also help spot the ball and then give the ready-for-play signal and sound the whistle. If the offensive team has made a first down or a change of team possession has occurred, give the time-out signal to stop the clock unless it has already been stopped by rule.

### *Umpire*

After the ball is spotted, remain over the ball until the referee gives the ready-for-play signal. You usually take a position 3 to 8 yards behind the defensive line and between the defensive ends, keeping the snap in view. You should not interfere with the vision or movement of defensive backs and should vary your position so that players cannot use you as interference. At this point, you should check

- the number of offensive players;
- the five players numbered 50 through 79 on the offensive line;
- interference with the snap, a false start or encroachment;
- disconcerting signals by the defense;
- the position of the ball between the inbounds lines and
- defensive players on the line of scrimmage in the free-blocking zone.

After the snap, you are responsible for keying the center and guards. If they block aggressively, read the run. If they pass block, read the pass. You should also read the point of attack, paying particular attention to free-blocking zone restrictions.

When the play is wide to the side, you should move in that direction, observing initial line play and action around the runner (especially on short gains or losses in side zones). Remain on the inside and work to the outside to maintain boxed-in coverage. When a hole opens directly in front of you, react and adjust according to the play, moving laterally from the hole and being alert for the tight end cutting across. You cover the action at the point of attack and then behind the runner. Check for illegal use of hands or arms and other fouls near the neutral zone. Be alert for the following:

- A quick kick or pass
- Ineligible receivers and the point the forward pass first strikes anything
- A fumble that occurs beyond the neutral zone; assist in determining who secures possession
- An illegal contact on the snapper
- Action of players in and just behind the neutral zone

You should not sound your whistle unless the covering official is not in position. Assist in spotting the ball and assist with the relay if the ball goes out of bounds.

### Linesman and Line Judge

After the ball is spotted, straddle the line the ball is on, no closer than 9 yards outside the widest offensive player, on the sideline if necessary. You then check the down-box number, look at each other through the line and signal the number of the down. Use an extended-arm signal and hold it until the snap to indicate that the closest offensive player is off the line of scrimmage. Then count defensive players and identify eligible receivers on your side. Be alert for illegal substitutions. You should check

- wingbacks, flankers, split ends and slot backs;
- the first two players in from your end of the offensive line, including backs, as eligible pass receivers;
- the player in motion away from you, maintaining responsibility for him if he reverses direction;
- a minimum of seven offensive players on the line of scrimmage and
- encroachment or a false start.

After the snap, key the end and the wide receiver if the defender is covering him tightly. If the end is uncovered, look through to the tackle to read the run or pass. You should also be alert for

- quick plays into the line and helping to mark forward progress with the downfield foot,
- initial charges of linemen,
- blocks near the neutral zone to the tackle on a wide end run to your side and
- blocks on eligible receivers.

When the ball comes to your side of the field, you should cover the sideline and watch for crackback blocks. Sound the whistle when the ball becomes dead and move to the spot of the ball. If the ball becomes dead in the side zone, toss it to the referee or umpire for spotting. When the ball goes to the opposite side, move cautiously into the general area until you are certain that there will be no reverse or counter. Observe action on the linebacker and back-side pursuit. On down-the-line option plays toward you, observe the pitchman, a possible loose ball and the pitchman as he becomes the runner.

Additionally, you observe late blocks and forearm blows away from the runner. You also are responsible for the entire sideline, so if the ball goes out of bounds, you must signal time-out immediately and hold the out-of-bounds spot while another official retrieves the ball. While moving downfield with the runner, watch for an illegal forward pass or fumble. If play continues following an illegal forward pass, drop a penalty marker at the spot of the pass to indicate where the run ended and at the spot of any subsequent foul. Do not sound your whistle.

When you work with the line-to-gain crew as the linesman, you have certain responsibilities and points of protocol to follow. You echo the referee's signal orally and with the proper hand signal. You also should repeat the referee's time-out signal. Do not turn your back on the field of play when you are having equipment moved. The authorized down marker should be moved only after the referee's signal.

When it is necessary to move the yardage chain, you should spot the foremost point of the ball with your downfield foot, have the down-box operator mark the spot, inform the referee that the yardage chain is ready and have the line-to-gain crew set the two rods.

### All Officials

All officials are responsible for keeping running plays properly boxed in. Before sounding the whistle, be certain that the ball is dead, know the location of the ball and keep your eyes on the runner when he is covering.

When the ball becomes dead in your area, sound your whistle promptly and be alert for dead-ball fouls, surprise plays or fumbles. If a fumble occurs, you, the covering official, should mark the spot of the fumble (not the spot where the fumble was recovered) with your beanbag and rule on possession immediately. If the defense recovers, immediately signal time-out and then signal first down. If the fumbling team recovers (the ball does not become dead automatically when recovered), indicate the number of the next down with your fingers or fist if it is fourth down. If the ball becomes dead before the fumble, sound your whistle immediately to indicate that the down has ended.

If the ball goes out of bounds, as the covering official you give the time-out signal immediately and mark and hold the spot while continuing to observe the action. The nearest free official retrieves the ball, unless you (the covering official) are in the best position to do so. All other officials echo the time-out signal and move quickly into position to assist in getting the ball ready for play. They should also be alert for substitution infractions.

## Forward Pass

As mentioned earlier, passing plays occur less frequently than running plays in high school football. But that is only a general tendency. Starting positions for passing plays are similar to those for running plays (see figure 3.4 on page 59).

Because gifted quarterbacks are the exception in high school football, a team that has one holds a distinct advantage. An official's lack of knowledge or inexperience in reacting to passing plays of all types should not negate that advantage.

Officials have more ground to cover on passing plays and more open-field activity to monitor. Officials must avoid being caught short. The rhythm and fairness of the game depends on the officials, whether a team throws once a game or 50 times a game. Following are responsibilities on passing plays.

### Referee

After the ball is spotted, declare the ball ready for play by positioning yourself behind the offensive team (in a position most advantageous to the situation). Vary your distance behind the formation and to the side with the offensive formation. You should be able to view the tackle on the far side and the backs. You should then count offensive players and identify eligible backs.

After the snap, read the block of the offensive tackle on the opposite side and observe all blocks behind the neutral zone. As the passer retreats, you should remain wide and deeper than the passer and give special attention to contact with the passer. After the passer releases the ball, continue to observe him, not the flight of the ball, and orally alert defenders that the passer has released the ball. At this point, you determine whether the pass was forward or backward. Be alert for illegal passes. When the passer approaches the neutral zone, move to the spot of the pass to determine whether the passer's feet were in or behind the neutral zone when he released the ball. If the pass was illegal, drop the penalty marker and continue to officiate. If the legality of the pass is in doubt, mark the spot of the pass with your beanbag and continue to officiate. At the completion of the down, examine the spot of the beanbag and throw a flag if the beanbag is beyond the neutral zone.

You are solely responsible for calling intentional grounding, but you may receive assistance from a covering official. Continue to observe the action behind the neutral zone before leaving the area. You are responsible for the runner until he crosses the neutral zone.

### Umpire

After the ball is spotted, position yourself 3 to 8 yards behind the defensive line and between the defensive ends, keeping the snap in view and remaining over the ball until the referee gives the ready-for-play signal. You should not interfere with the vision or movement of defensive backs. Vary your position so that players cannot use you for interference, and note the defensive players on the line of scrimmage in the free-blocking zone.

After the snap, you should be alert for illegal contact on the snapper. Watch for illegal use of hands by offensive linemen. When you read a forward pass, stepping to the neutral zone will remove you as a target on shallow drag passes and put you in position to rule on whether an ineligible player is illegally downfield.

Additionally, you should observe the action of players in and just behind the neutral zone and assist the referee in determining whether the passer's feet were in or behind the neutral zone when he released the ball. Drop the penalty marker at the spot from which an illegal pass is thrown, cover short passes down the middle, know where a forward pass first touches anything and cover fumbled passes in your area and mark the spot.

### Linesman and Line Judge

After the ball is spotted, take the same position that you do for a running play on your respective sideline. As a linesman or line judge, you assist with the lineup. The linesman checks the down-box number and signals to the referee the number of the down. The line judge is alert for illegal substitutions, counts defensive players and identifies eligible receivers. Both should use the extended-arm signal and hold it until the snap to indicate that the closest offensive player is off the line of scrimmage. Both should be alert for a player in motion away from them and maintain responsibility for him if he reverses direction.

After the snap, key through the end to read the initial block of the tackle and move to a position to check blocking and contact of eligible receivers and linebackers. Be ready to rule on the direction of a quick quarterback pass and move cautiously downfield 5 to 7 yards, approximately halfway between that zone and the deepest receiver to watch for interference by either team and to rule on a fumble or an illegal pass after a completion.

If a pass is incomplete in your area, sound your whistle, give the incomplete-pass signal, retrieve the ball and relay it to the official nearest the previous spot. As the linesman or line judge, you must be ready to adjust coverage if a potential passer decides to run. Be alert for sideline action and for forward progress of the runner.

Additionally, you are responsible for the entire sideline and should always be prepared to come back to rule on a play near the neutral zone.

### Covering Officials

Be alert for an illegal pass and watch for touching or catching by an ineligible player. The ball stays live. Also watch for holding of eligible receivers and all contact beyond the neutral zone, both before and after the pass is thrown.

If you are ruling on a pass reception involving the sideline, you should only use a signal governing the action. If a pass is intercepted inside the defensive team's 5-yard line and the player making the interception is downed in the end zone or the ball goes out of bounds, be prepared to rule whether the player's momentum took him into the end zone. Mark the spot of the interception with your beanbag.

## Goal-Line Play

To officials, goal-line plays are the same as any other play from scrimmage (see figure 3.5). In fact, they are identical before the snap. The differences come in when determining whether a team has scored and then taking the proper action.

Goal-line plays can be a chaotic time for players and coaches. Officials, however, should remain composed. Additional emotion or exaggerated signals are unnecessary.

As an official on the goal line, you make subtle mechanical adjustments, but your demeanor should be the same as it is at midfield. Following are the mechanics of the goal-line situation.

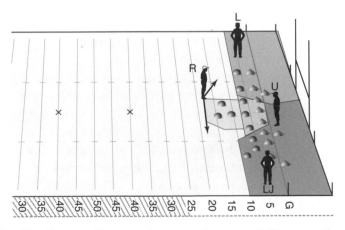

**FIGURE 3.5**   Starting positions and areas of responsibility near the goal line.

### Referee

As the referee, you should position yourself and cover the same way you do for any scrimmage play. Give the touchdown signal if another official has signaled a touchdown and no foul has occurred. Do not give the touchdown signal from behind the runner unless the score is obvious.

### Umpire

As the umpire for a goal-line play, you should position yourself near the goal line and use the same coverage you use for any scrimmage play. When the runner has made a quick thrust into the line, be sure that the ball is not moved forward after it is declared dead. Assist the wing official if he needs help. Do not give the touchdown signal from in front of the runner unless the score is obvious. In most crews the umpire does not give the touchdown signal.

### Linesman and Line Judge

As the linesman or line judge for a goal-line play, you position yourself as you would for any scrimmage play. On a snap between the 10- and 5-yard lines, release slowly downfield and stay ahead of the runner to the goal line. On a snap inside the 5-yard line, release to the goal line and officiate back to the ball. Note the farthest point to which the offensive team advances the ball:

- If the ball is short of the goal line, move in quickly and help by marking the point with the downfield foot.
- If you see the runner who is in possession of the ball touch or cross the goal-line plane, instantly give the touchdown signal.

As the linesman, you are also responsible to see that the clip on the chain is at the intersection with the goal line before the line-to-gain chains are moved off the sideline. You should remove the line-to-gain equipment from the sideline when the line to gain is the goal line. Both the linesman and line judge should straddle the goal-line pylon.

### All Officials

For a goal-line play, only the official or officials who see the touchdown should give the touchdown signal. Officials who do not observe the touchdown do not mirror the signal.

## Scrimmage Kicks

A scrimmage kick is a tricky play for officials because of the variety of situations that can arise depending on the length of the kick, side of the field the ball is kicked to, length of the return, blocked kick possibilities and so on. See figure 3.6 for proper positioning.

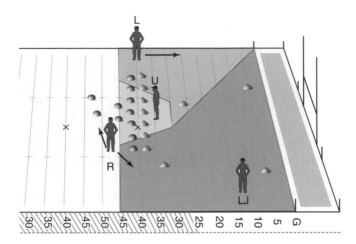

FIGURE 3.6   Starting positions and areas of responsibility on a scrimmage kick.

In addition, a scrimmage kick combines the responsibilities of a play from scrimmage and a kick; two distinctly different activities occur during the same play. A smooth transition between the two is crucial, and executing it is difficult. If an official becomes bogged down with his scrimmage responsibilities, he will have difficulty recovering to take care of the open-field action of a kick return. Likewise, if an official takes on kicking responsibilities too early, he will not perform line-of-scrimmage duties properly. Adhering to the following scrimmage kick mechanics will reduce these difficulties.

### Referee

After the ball is spotted, your position as the referee is 3 to 4 yards in advance of and 5 to 7 yards outside the player in the kicker's position, on the line judge's side of the field. You should check down and distance with the linesman and declare the ball ready for play by using established procedure. Count the kicking team's players.

After the snap, watch for fouls behind the neutral zone, especially near the kicker. Also be alert for a blocked kick and be ready to rule on the recovery. After the ball crosses the neutral zone, observe line play and move downfield slowly following the kick. Watch for fouls and be ready to pick up the runner if a long return occurs. Also determine from the covering official if the ball was touched beyond neutral zone and by whom.

Be prepared for kicks out of bounds in flight. For a long kick, move to the spot of the kick (spot of the kicker), and then line up the covering official on the spot where the ball crossed the sideline by using an outstretched arm. For a short kick, go directly to the out-of-bounds spot.

If no foul occurs, signal the linesman to move the line-to-gain equipment. Obtain the ready sign from the linesman before giving the ready-for-play signal.

### Umpire

After the ball is spotted, your position as the umpire is 4 to 7 yards deep, keeping the ball in view. You count the punting team's players and check numbering exceptions. Key on the offensive guards and center. You will focus on and rule on the legality of the snap.

After the snap, step toward the neutral zone and be alert for roughing the snapper. Then shift to the action of the offensive guards and the backs behind the neutral zone. You should read the play and be alert for a fake punt—either a run or a pass. You should also be prepared to assist the referee in covering a short or blocked kick and be responsible for determining if the ball crosses the neutral zone.

After the kick, pivot to view the line judge's side of the field to observe blocks in the side zone. Move toward the return area, observing players away from the ball. Be alert for fouls in the secondary and move downfield slowly. If the ball goes out of bounds, move to help relay the ball to the inbounds spot.

### Linesman

After the ball is spotted, your position as the linesman is the same as it would be for a run or pass, straddling the line of scrimmage not closer than 9 yards outside the widest offensive player. Then check the down number and count the returning team's players. After the referee declares the ball ready for play, you are responsible for the neutral zone.

After the snap, cover all kicks to your side. If the ball goes out of bounds in flight, sound your whistle and give the time-out signal. Move farther downfield than where the ball went out of bounds and walk upfield until the referee spots you on the sideline.

If the ball rolls out of bounds, sound the whistle and give the time-out signal. Hold the spot, drop your beanbag at the spot if the ball must be retrieved and continue to observe the action. Assist the referee in covering the ball on a short or blocked kick by noting if the kick is touched beyond the neutral zone or recovered in or behind the neutral zone. Carry your beanbag in your hand during the down to mark first touching, a fumble, momentum or the end of a kick. If a fair-catch signal is made, you must observe if the signaler blocks.

Watch for clipping and other fouls in the secondary. Move with the runner if he comes to your side, and follow him to the goal line if he breaks the run.

When the ball becomes dead, sound your whistle, give the time-out signal and mark the spot. Make sure of possession on a fair catch. If a foul occurs, the free official should cover the ball while the official who had the foul reports the information to the referee. Watch the referee for the signal to move the line-to-gain equipment.

### Line Judge

After the ball is spotted, your position as the line judge is 7 to 10 yards wider than and in front of the deepest receiver, in position to cover the sideline as well as the kick and count the returning team's players.

After the snap, carry your beanbag in your hand during the down to mark first touching, fumble momentum or end of the kick. You are also responsible for the initial action on or by the end on your side. Cover all kicks down the middle and to your side.

If the ball rolls out of bounds, sound the whistle, give the time-out signal, hold the spot and continue to observe the action. Drop your beanbag at the spot if the ball must be retrieved. If the ball goes out of bounds in flight, sound the whistle and give the time-out signal. You should go deeper than the spot where the ball went out of bounds and walk back toward the referee. Have the referee spot you on the sideline. Hold the spot until the ball has been spotted for the next down.

If the ball stays inbounds, be ready to rule on whether either team touched the kick. If the ball is muffed, be prepared to rule on possession. Be alert for a handoff or a reverse. If the kicking team is first to touch a moving kick, mark the spot of the first touching with a beanbag and continue to cover the play. If the kicking team is first to touch the kick at rest beyond the neutral zone, sound your whistle, give the time-out signal and mark the spot.

Following a fair catch, sound your whistle, give the time-out signal, mark the spot and observe the action of the signaler. When no fair catch is made, be prepared to rule on a touchback or safety or whether the receiver's momentum took him into end zone.

When the kick is returned, move with the runner if he runs up the middle or to your side until another official picks him up. After doing that, delay and observe the action behind the ball. When the kick becomes dead, sound the whistle immediately and give the time-out signal. Inform the referee of ball status before placing it for the next play.

If the kick is caught inside the 5-yard line and the player is downed in his end zone or the ball goes out of bounds there, be prepared to rule on whether the player's momentum took him into end zone. Mark the spot of the catch inside the 5-yard line with your beanbag.

# Field-Goal Attempts

Like a punting situation, a field-goal attempt is a hybrid between a play from scrimmage and a kick. Although returns are not the norm, they are within the rules and occur occasionally in high school football—particularly on long field-goal attempts. Officials must stay alert if the attempt is particularly short and in the field of play.

Field-goal attempts on either side of the 15-yard line include subtle differences of responsibilities, depending on the crew member. This section covers guidelines for responsibilities from all distances.

## Field-Goal Attempts for Ball Snapped From 15-Yard Line or Closer

Responsibilities for field-goal attempts from the 15-yard line or closer (see figure 3.7) are similar for a kick attempt of any distance, but a couple minor differences should be noted. Most notably, the referee makes the signal of whether the kick is good.

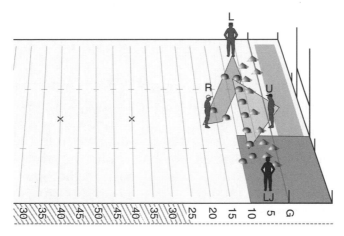

FIGURE 3.7   Starting positions and areas of responsibility on a field goal from the 15-yard line or closer.

### *Referee*

After the ball is spotted, position yourself at about a 45-degree angle about 1 yard to the rear and at least 2 to 3 yards to the side of the potential kicker. You should be able to see the face of the holder and should be in a position where you can see the holder receive the ball. Count the kicking team's players and rule on the motion of backs within your line of vision.

After the snap, watch for a muff or fumble by the holder and be alert for a run or pass. If the ball is kicked, move quickly behind the kicker into the line of flight of the ball. Rule on the kick after getting the signal from the line judge about whether the ball passed over the crossbar. Signal score or no score. If a try is blocked, immediately sound your whistle and give the no-score signal. If a field goal is blocked, the ball remains live.

### Umpire

After the ball is spotted, position yourself 5 to 7 yards deep, keeping the ball in view. Check for the use of numbering exceptions and keys on the action of the center and guards.

After the snap, step toward the neutral zone, reading the interior linemen. Check the action on the snapper and be alert for a kick crossing the neutral zone, a short kick or a blocked kick. Following the kick, pivot to view the line-judge side of the field to observe blocks in the side zone. Then move downfield watching the action away from the ball.

### Linesman

After the ball is spotted, take a position 9 yards outside the offensive end and observe the neutral zone.

After the snap, read the end and tackle and be alert for a fake kick—either a run or a pass. If the ball is kicked, move into the kicking team's backfield and watch for roughing the kicker or holder.

### Line Judge

After the ball is spotted, position yourself 9 yards outside the offensive end and count the defensive players. Handle this play as you would any goal-line play.

After the snap, read the offensive end and move to the end line to determine whether the ball passes over or under the crossbar. If the ball passes under the crossbar, immediately signal no score. Sound the whistle when a successful kick passes through the uprights or when the kick is apparently unsuccessful after breaking the goal-line plane.

## Field-Goal Attempts for Ball Snapped Outside 15-Yard Line

One main difference in responsibility on longer field-goal attempts (see figure 3.8) is that the referee does not make the official call on whether the kick is successful. On attempts in which the ball is snapped outside the 15-yard line, the line judge makes the call and the referee simply mimics the call of the line judge to the press box.

### Referee

Take the same position that you would for a snap inside the 15-yard line—looking at the face of the holder from a position about 1 yard behind and at least 2 to 3 yards to the side of the kicker and at about a 45-degree angle. Cover as you would cover any scrimmage kick. You're also responsible for the kicker and holder after the snap.

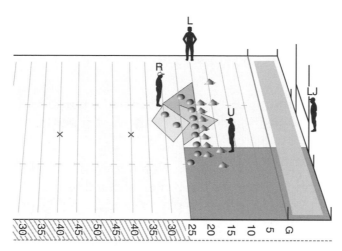

FIGURE 3.8    Starting positions on field-goal attempts from outside the 15-yard line.

### Umpire

Position yourself as you would for a snap inside the 15-yard line—5 to 7 yards off the line, favoring the line judge's side of the field. Cover as you would cover any scrimmage kick.

### Linesman

Position yourself by moving downfield as you would for any scrimmage kick. Straddle the line of scrimmage, not closer than 9 yards outside the widest offensive player, and cover the line of scrimmage to the end line.

### Line Judge

Take a position 5 yards behind and directly between the uprights. Rule on whether the kick is successful or unsuccessful, and give the appropriate signal. If the kick is unsuccessful, rule on a possible touchback. You're also responsible for the sideline and end line on runs and passes.

# After Touchbacks, Safeties, Tries or Field-Goal Attempts

Touchbacks, safeties, tries and field-goal attempts are four distinct plays. Each involves its own set of responsibilities that officials must carry out. But after completion of any of the plays, postplay duties are identical. The officials' positioning is a little different, depending on the play, but the responsibilities are the same.

### Referee

Declare the ball ready for play, count the kicking or offensive team's players and be alert for illegal substitutions.

### Umpire

Be alert for substitutions and irregularities in the number of players. You will move to your position and will count the proper team.

### Linesman

Take the ball to the center of the field on the proper yard line and place it with the foremost point on the center of the line. You also count the defensive or kick-receiving team's players and are alert for substitutions. Then hand the ball to the kicker if it is put in play by a free kick. Instruct the kicker to wait for the referee's signal and then move to the sideline where the line-to-gain equipment is located.

### Line Judge

As line judge, you retrieve any kicked ball. If a kickoff is to follow, the down-box operator should retrieve the ball and relay it to you; in turn, you relay it to the linesman. You also count players on the proper team and are alert for substitutions.

### All Officials

All officials are alert for substitutions and irregularities in the number of players. Officials should not permit team attendants on the field following a touchback. Officials should strive to put the ball in play immediately.

As a reminder, on free kicks following a safety, each official assumes the same relative position and has the same duties as they do on kickoffs, except the kicking team's free-kick line becomes the 20-yard line instead of the 40-yard line (see figure 3.9). The ball may be put in play by a punt, place kick or drop kick.

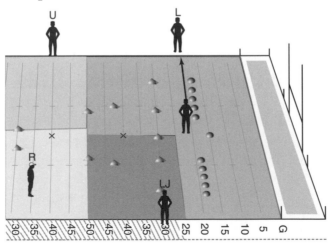

FIGURE 3.9   Starting positions on a free kick after a safety.

# Administrative Duties

Following are procedures or techniques that deal with officials' reactions to various game circumstances, including enforcing penalties after infractions; measuring for first downs and carrying out procedures for time-outs, ends of periods, between periods and between halves.

You should not consider these tasks "extra" duties or "throw-in" responsibilities. Quick administration of these procedures keeps the game moving. Undue delays impair the flow of a football game. If you know what to do and when to do it, you can keep things moving along.

## Enforcing the Rules

A common mistake for a new official is to consider throwing the flag his primary responsibility. Certainly, it's important to enforce the rules and administer penalties. But it's just as important to remember that you are not part of the show. Your job is to enforce rules, enhance safety and keep the game flowing. Call infractions and administer penalties but don't become caught up in it. Remain professional and unemotional. If players or coaches break a rule, take action and move on.

### Referee

When the ball is dead following a foul, give the time-out signal and obtain full information from the official who called the foul.

Generally, the umpire is in the center of the field and will "march off" the penalty, if accepted. As the referee, you may be on or near a sideline on the opposite side of the field from the official who threw the flag. The official who threw the flag can move to the umpire quicker than he can move to the referee. The two sideline officials (linesman and line judge) can learn from the umpire the nature of the foul and tell their respective coaches.

As the referee, you then give a preliminary signal to the press-box side of the field only and give options to the captain of the offended team. When the captain's most advantageous choice is obvious, quickly inform him of the options. If he does not respond, consider his silence acceptance of the obvious choice. After the captain has made a choice, he cannot revoke it.

Make note of the enforcement spot for the penalty and confirm the yardage with the umpire. After the ball has been spotted, give the final signal for the foul to the press-box side of the field only.

If the penalty is declined, go to the spot of the ball and give the foul signal and then the penalty-declined signal to the press box. When a double foul occurs, signal each foul, facing the press box. You should follow the foul signals with a penalty-declined signal. When enforcing two penalties, give proper signals following each enforcement. When the penalty is to be enforced on the kickoff, indicate the scoring signal, follow with the proper foul signal, point to the offending team and point toward the succeeding spot. After an accepted penalty for a foul by either team during the last timed down of a period, play continues with an untimed down.

### Umpire

Secure the ball, make note of the enforcement spot for the penalty and proceed with measurement. On a properly marked field, avoid stepping off the distance between yard lines, except to the first yard line and for the final yard line. Walk briskly, using an arm signal to point to each yard line you cross.

### Linesman

You should be certain of the down number and go to the succeeding spot. Be ready to have the line-to-gain equipment moved after penalty administration. Give the final signal for the foul to be enforced on a kickoff to the press-box side of the field. You also assist the line judge in checking enforcement and in keeping trainers, attendants or coaches from coming onto the field.

### Line Judge

Return the time-out signal to the referee and hold the enforcement spot. As the line judge, you also assist the linesman in checking enforcement and in keeping trainers, attendants or coaches from coming onto the field.

### All Officials

All officials observe live-ball fouls, withhold the whistle, drop a penalty marker at the proper yard line and continue to observe the play, noting the location of the ball at the time of the foul.

When the ball becomes dead, give the time-out signal and sound the whistle but give no visible signal. Report this information orally to the referee. You should make a mental note about whether the clock should be started on ready or on the snap. Remind the referee whether or not the clock will start with the ready.

When observing a dead-ball foul, sound the whistle, toss a penalty marker into the air and give the time-out signal immediately. Then report the information orally to the referee and make sure that the umpire assesses the penalty properly in all respects.

After you've called a foul and the ball has been declared dead, sound the whistle, stop the clock and get the referee's attention by giving short blasts of the whistle. As the calling official, you should make sure that another official is covering the spot of the foul and orally report full information to the referee and umpire. As the calling official, you must

- identify the foul;

- identify the offending team including jersey color and offense or defense, or kicking or receiving team;
- identify the offending player's number or position;
- indicate the spot of the foul, end of the run or end of the kick and
- indicate the status of the ball when the foul occurred.

You also assist with locating captains and recovering penalty markers and the ball.

For enforcement, stay clear of the spot of the foul. If the enforcement spot is different from the spot of the foul, then go to the enforcement spot. When the umpire begins enforcement, other officials check for correctness and distance. They should avoid visiting while the penalty is assessed.

When an official calls a disqualifying foul, he informs the offending player and reports his number and the type of infraction to the referee, coach and other members of the officiating crew. The official should emphasize that the disqualification is for the remainder of the game. In the case of a double disqualifying foul, the referee may designate another official to assist in reporting the foul to the coaches. In addition, the official shall not place a hand on the offending player or accompany or escort him to the sideline. Other officials record the player's number and name, if known, and observe all other players. After the contest, the referee should notify the state association if applicable and report unsportsmanlike penalties.

## First-Down Measurements

The following techniques and procedures should be applied when measuring for first downs using the traditional rods and chain. Once the ball is declared dead in a specific spot and it is determined that a first-down measurement is needed, the officials should measure for a first down as shown in figure 3.10. If another method is being used, officials must be

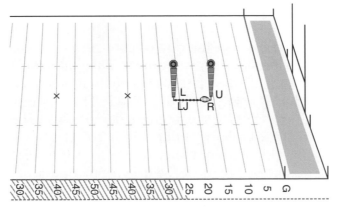

FIGURE 3.10 Officials' positions on a first-down measurement.

aware of it before the game begins and discuss the methodology with the line-to-gain crew. Stress to the "chain gang" the importance of getting on and off the field quickly. Nothing slows a game more than confusion or uncertainty on every measurement.

### Referee

You give the time-out signal and signal the linesman to bring the chain onto the field. You should then motion players away from the ball. Rotate the ball so that the long axis is parallel to the sideline (see figure 3.11, a-c). In a side zone, measure before the ball is taken to the inbounds line.

If the line to gain does not reach the side zone, use the chain to place the ball accurately at the inbounds spot. If the ball has gone out of bounds, measure to the point where the ball crossed the sideline (remember that the inside edge of the forward rod marks the line to gain). When measurement is complete, signal the number of the next down, spot the ball at the proper place and wait for the line-to-gain crew to return to position.

If a new series is awarded to the opponent of the team that was in possession when the ball became dead, place the ball so that the foremost point when it became dead becomes the rear point for the new direction. Set the new rear rod with the inside edge at the new point of the ball so that the line to gain is 10 yards in advance of that point.

After measurement, get ready signs from the captains and declare the ball ready for play by using established procedure. If the ball was not out of bounds, signal the clock to start with your declaration of ready for play. If the ball turns over on downs, start the clock on the snap.

### Umpire

Take the forward rod from the chainman at the place of measurement. When the linesman says, "Ready," tighten the chain and hold the forward rod near the ball until the referee reaches a decision.

### Linesman

When the referee signals a measurement, grasp both the chain and the clip at the back edge of the back yard line (not just grasping the clip because it could detach) and instruct the down-box operator to mark the front rod spot and keep the same down number. Then take the chain behind the ball and place the clipped part of the chain at the back edge of the back yard line. Hold it firmly and call, "Ready" to the umpire to stretch the chain tight. Then wait for the referee's decision and signal.

If the location of the ball does not result in a first down, you should, while holding the chain, accompany the crew to the sideline, reset in the original position and request the down-box operator to move the indicator to the next down. If the location of the ball results in a new

FIGURE 3.11 Measure a first down by (*a*) determining that the ball is dead, (*b*) determining the position of the ball's forward point and (*c*) placing the long axis of the ball parallel to the sideline.

series, drop the chain and, when the chain gang reaches the sideline, set the inside edge of the rear rod at the foremost point of the ball after the referee spots it. First down should be on the marker. Mark the foremost point of the ball for the down-marker operator on all first downs.

### Line Judge

Take a position behind the yard line from which the measurement will be made and align the linesman with the ball so that the measurement is accurate. You should not permit team attendants to enter the field.

## Conventional Time-Outs

Quick recognition by officials and a clear signal to the game-clock operator are the two most important factors in executing a conventional time-out. Staying abreast of the game situation leads to awareness that a time-out is likely and enhances sharpness. Officials must stay alert. Proper, expedient time-out calls can be the difference in a football game. Officials must avoid becoming the difference.

### Referee

You sound the whistle and signal time-out. If the time-out is charged to a team, you indicate that by moving both arms three times in a horizontal motion toward that team. To indicate an official's time-out, tap your chest with both hands.

As referee, your main duties during a time-out are to check the number of time-outs remaining for each team, check the time remaining with the line judge and check the down with the linesman. You also notify the coach and captain after a third time-out has been charged. You then take a position away from the other officials and observe the defense.

Time a 60-second interval. At 45 seconds, signal the linesman and line judge by pointing directly at them to give their teams a 15-second warning. Inform each team's huddle of the down and the time remaining in the period. Declare the ball ready for play by using established procedure.

### Umpire

Maintain a position over the ball and observe the offense, making sure that the proper personnel are on the field and that they are using only proper and legal communication (for example, players cannot wear headsets to communicate with the press box). Continue to monitor the offense until the referee is ready to start play.

### Linesman and Line Judge

As the linesman or line judge, you move to position halfway between the ball and the sideline. Be alert for the signal from the referee to give teams the 15-second warning. Go to your respective team huddle and say, "Coach, the ball will be ready for play in fifteen seconds."

Be alert for substitutions by the teams on your sideline or attempts by the team to use substitutes for the purpose of deception. Maintain the proper number of players and attendants in the huddle when conferences are held between the inbounds lines. Inform the captain and coach of the number of time-outs remaining.

### All Officials

All officials repeat the time-out signal and record the time-out, the number of the player who called it, the time on the clock and the period. You should stand alertly erect and not visit with players. Restrict any discussion to captains only. You should not huddle in a group with other officials.

## Injury Time-Outs

Following are additional responsibilities for injury time-outs beyond regular time-out duties.

### Referee

During an injury time-out, you summon the trainer or trainers or one or more coaches onto the field. Your main duties at this point are to determine whether the injured player is or was unconscious and, if so, to inform the coach that the player may not return to the game without written approval from a physician. Be ready to assist the trainer or coaches in securing additional medical help, if needed. Continue to observe other players and allow clear access to the injured player.

As referee, you should also attempt to keep players a significant distance away from the seriously injured player or players. Direct players and coaches toward their respective team-bench areas. After the medical staff begins to work on an injured player, all members of the officiating crew should control the total playing-field environment and team personnel and allow the medical staff to perform services without interruption or interference. Officials should always ensure adequate lines of vision between the medical staff and available emergency personnel.

The officiating crew should control players and coaches so that they do not interfere with medical services performed by the athletic trainers or team physicians or complain about the time taken to perform such services.

### Umpire

Make sure that the summoned trainer or trainers or coaches are not on the field for coaching purposes.

## End-of-Period Procedure

The end-of-period procedure is a basic process, particularly when field clocks are readily visible. Officials must be aware when time is running out and make sure that no play begins after the clock ticks to zero (both for safety and for the officials' credibility).

### Referee

If a field clock is not used or has become disabled, take an official's time-out with approximately four minutes remaining in the second and fourth periods, inform both captains of the time remaining and see that both coaches are notified.

When time expires, the ball becomes dead. Sound the whistle and give the time-out signal. If a field clock is used, you (when facing the clock) are responsible for knowing when time expires. If time expires before a snap, sound your whistle to prevent the snap, if possible. If the ball is snapped immediately after time expires, sound your whistle loud and long and give the time-out signal.

After a delay to ensure that no foul, no obvious timing error, no request for a coach-referee conference or no other irregularity has occurred, hold the ball in one hand over your head to signal the official end of the period.

### Umpire

If a field clock is used, you (when facing the clock) are responsible for knowing when time expires. If time expires before the snap, sound the whistle to prevent the snap, if possible. If the ball is snapped immediately after time expires, sound the whistle loud and long and give the time-out signal.

### Line Judge

If a field clock is not used, you keep the official time. Notify the referee approximately four minutes before the end of the second and fourth periods. You also notify the referee approximately 30 seconds before the end of the period that time may expire during the next down. When time expires and the ball becomes dead, you signal the referee by raising an arm above your head. You sound the whistle and give the time-out signal.

## Between Periods

Officials should make sure that both teams agree with the officiating crew about the length of time between periods. All parties must know in advance how much time they have between periods. The duration of the break should be established long before the period ends. Scrambling should not be necessary. As an official, you should stay organized. You have plenty of time to respot the ball.

### Referee

Time a one-minute interval, as you would in the standard time-out procedure, including signaling the linesman and line judge to give their teams a 15-second warning. Note and record the down, distance and yard line nearest the foremost point of the ball. You should announce this information to other officials and confirm it with the linesman and umpire. As the referee, you also measure the distance from the nearest yard line to the foremost point of the ball and estimate the distance from the inbounds line. In spotting the ball, you should check again with the linesman and umpire.

At the end of 60 seconds while near the ball, announce the down and distance and declare the ball ready for play by using established procedure.

### Umpire

Record the down, distance and yard line nearest the foremost point of the ball and assist the referee. Take the ball quickly to the corresponding point on the other half of the field and reverse its direction. You should also review the correct yard line and inbounds spot with the linesman and chain position.

### Linesman

Record the down, distance and yard line nearest the foremost point of the ball, confirm the information with the referee and grasp the chain and the clip, which is near the back stake. Note that the clip should have been attached to the chain at the beginning of the series of downs. You also call the down and distance to the assistants. Reverse ends of the yardage chain (pointing in the same direction as the offense is now headed after the change of quarter) and set the yardage chain after the referee spots the ball. You then check the number of the down and the distance to gain.

You assume the responsibilities outlined for a conventional time-out, including giving your team a 15-second warning when directed by the referee. As the linesman, you indicate to the referee that he is ready by signaling the number of the down with your fingers, or your fist, for fourth down.

### Line Judge

Observe the teams while moving to the corresponding spot on the other end of the field and assume the responsibilities outlined for a standard time-out, including giving your team a 15-second warning when directed by the referee. Also check the team box and huddle areas for appropriate conference procedure, as permitted during a charged time-out.

### All Officials

Between periods, no more than three team attendants are permitted on the field. At this time, either legal type of coach-player conference may be held.

## Between Halves

The procedure between halves is much the same as the procedure between periods, although there are a few important differences. Again, communication is the key, particularly because teams often assemble at halftime away from the field and away from the officials. Everyone should be aware of halftime procedures well before halftime.

Additionally, all officials should leave the field together and assemble in the dressing room or other private place. At this point, they discuss overtime procedure, if applicable. They return to the field at least five minutes before the second half is to begin. They should start the second half on time.

### Referee

Instruct the time operator to time the intermission and signal when it is time to start the clock. At the conclusion of the halftime intermission, you are responsible for seeing that three minutes is placed on the clock for the mandatory warm-up period before the start of the second half after the intermission time elapses. Remember not to visit with anyone and only discuss situations with officials in the dressing room or another private place.

You then give the game ball to the linesman and determine which team has the choice for the second half. Escort the captain to the center of the field and relay the choices to the team bench and press box with appropriate signals.

### Umpire and Line Judge

As the umpire to begin the second half, escort the captains to the center of the field. As a line judge, take a position on the sideline opposite the line-to-gain crew. As the umpire, move to the sideline near the 20-yard line opposite the linesman.

### Linesman

During intermission, discuss with the line-to-gain crew any aspects of their duties that they might improve to aid in game administration.

In preparing for the second half, station the line-to-gain crew near the team box and on the receiving team's end of the field. Also secure the game ball, hand it to the kicker and instruct him to wait for the referee's signal before he kicks. Then move to the sideline on the kicking team's free-kick line.

# CHAPTER 4

# Five-Person Crew Mechanics

In this chapter of *Officiating Football*, we deal with officials' responsibilities when working in a five-person crew. You will learn about positioning before plays, reading the proper keys and what reactions you should make—from kickoff through plays from scrimmage to end-of-game activities.

Remember that you should strive to have a thorough understanding of all officials' responsibilities on every play and in every situation, whether working on a four-person crew or a five-person crew. Even if your state association uses a five-person crew, you should become knowledgeable about the responsibilities of a four-person crew. That way, if one official fails to show up, or if a four-person crew is used for any other reason, you won't be caught short.

Some of the differences between a four- and five-person crew are subtle, but knowing the differences is important so that all officials will be on the same page from start to finish. If you're in a five-person crew, here are the mechanics you need to know.

## Kickoff

Officials should realize that teams employ strategies for kickoffs just as they do on plays from scrimmage. The more you know about these strategies before you move into position for the kickoff (see figure 4.1), the more prepared you will be to officiate the action. The kickoff requires officials to cover more territory than they do for any other play in football.

Each official has prekick responsibilities and performs different duties for kicks down the middle of the field, for long kicks and for onside kicks. Each official also covers different zones of the field. Individual officials must stick to their areas of responsibility to achieve full-field coverage. Officials working in four- and five-person crews have different

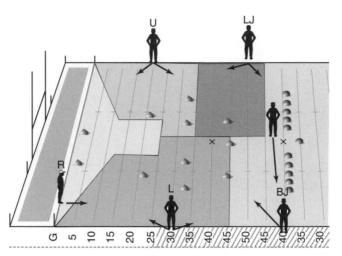

FIGURE 4.1    Starting positions and areas of responsibility on the kickoff.

responsibilities. Knowing both will allow you to officiate effectively in either situation. Following are the responsibilities when working in a five-person crew.

### Referee

Before the kick, your position as the referee is on the receiving team's goal line on the linesman's side near the inbounds line. Count the receiving team's players. Check the positions of the other officials and hold your arm above your head to request the ready sign from the other officials and the kicker. After you have received the ready sign, drop your arm and sound the whistle to signal the kicker to kick.

You must be prepared for several different types of kicks and be aware of your duties for each. Following are your duties for the types of kicks that may occur:

- *Short free kick.* Take a position near the receiving team's 10-yard line. You must be ready to assist other officials.

- *Kick down the middle.* Signal the clock to start when the kick is touched other than the first touching by the kicking team. Pick up the runner and follow him until releasing him to the covering official upfield.

- *Deep kick.* Retreat to the goal line to rule on a touchback. If a player catches the kick inside the 5-yard line and is downed in end zone or if the ball goes out of bounds there, mark the spot of the catch with your beanbag and rule on whether the player's momentum took him into the end zone.

- *Kick outside the opposite inbounds lines.* Move cautiously with the play and observe the action of other players near the runner. You serve as the cleanup behind, to the side of and around the runner.

- *Kick out of bounds.* Determine whether the receiving team touched or last touched the ball inbounds.

### Umpire

Before the kick, position yourself on the receiving team's 20-yard line on the sideline opposite the linesman. You should be certain that coaches, players, substitutes and other individuals are in their proper locations. Count the receiving team's players and then hold your arm above your head to indicate that you are ready. If you expect a short kick, take a position on the receiving team's 45-yard line.

After the kick, be aware of several different types of kicks. For a kick to your side, pick up the runner and follow him. When the kickoff goes outside the opposite inbounds line, move cautiously toward the play, observe the action of other players near the runner and serve as the cleanup behind, to the side of and around the runner. Maintain your position, preserving coverage of your sideline at all times. Mark the out-of-bounds spot if the kick goes out of bounds in your area. Use a beanbag if the receiving team last touched the ball inbounds or a penalty marker if the receiving team did not touch the ball inbounds.

### Linesman

As the linesman, take a position on the receiving team's 30-yard line on the sideline opposite the umpire. Before the kick, monitor the bench area and be certain that coaches, players, substitutes and other individuals are in proper locations. You then count the receiving team's players and hold your arm above your head to indicate that you are ready.

You should be prepared for several different types of kicks and must be aware of your duties for each. For all kicks, be alert for first touching by the kicking team and mark the spot with a beanbag. You should maintain a position that enables coverage of your sideline at all times. Additionally, observe the legality of blocks and action away from the ball when you are not covering the runner. Following are examples of your duties for the types of kicks that may occur:

- *Short free kick.* Take a position near the receiving team's free-kick line and be alert for the first touching by the kicking team or a kick that does not cross the receiving team's free-kick line. Hold your beanbag to mark the first touching by the kicking team.
- *Kick to your side.* Pick up the runner and follow him. When the ball becomes dead, sound the whistle and give the time-out signal. When applicable, mark the spot where the kick goes out of bounds on your side of field with a beanbag if touched inbounds by the receiving

team. Throw the penalty marker into the air if the receiving team does not touch the ball inbounds.

- *Kick to the opposite side of the field.* Move cautiously toward the play and observe the action of other players near the runner.

### Line Judge

As the line judge, you should be certain that coaches, players, substitutes and other individuals are in proper locations before the kick. Your position is on the receiving team's free-kick line, outside the sideline and opposite the linesman. Count the receiving team's players and identify the free-kick line for the receiving team. Hold your arm above your head to indicate that you are ready. Watch for any infractions involving the receiving team's free-kick line.

If you expect a short free kick, take a position on the receiving team's free-kick line and be alert for the first touching by the kicking team or a kick that does not cross the receiving team's free-kick line. You should hold your beanbag to mark the spot of the first touching by the kicking team.

After the kick, be alert for the first touching by the kicking team, mark that spot by dropping the beanbag on the proper yard line and watch the initial blocks in your area. If the ball becomes dead in your area, sound the whistle and give the time-out signal. Mark the spot where the kick goes out of bounds on your side of the field with the beanbag and throw your flag into the air if the receiving team does not touch it inbounds. After the ball has gone downfield, move deliberately in that direction while watching for fouls away from the ball. Cover 15 yards down the field along the sideline.

### Back Judge

As the back judge, take charge of the ball before the kick and position yourself on the kicking team's free-kick line in the side zone to monitor the bench area and assist the kicking team in getting into position. Move onto the field to the kicker and after checking the legality of the kicking tee, hand the ball to the kicker, point out the referee and instruct the kicker to wait for the referee's signal before kicking. Count the kicking team's players. Then move to a position just outside the sideline on the kicking team's free-kick line on the side where the line-to-gain equipment is located. Be certain that coaches, players, substitutes and other individuals are in proper locations. Hold your arm above your head to indicate that you are ready. You are responsible for the 25-second clock. Additionally, watch for any infractions involving the kicking team's free-kick line. If a dead-ball foul occurs, administer the penalty and place the ball ready.

After the kick, be alert for first touching by the kicking team and mark the spot with a beanbag. You should also be alert for a kick that does not cross the receiving team's free-kick line. If a penalty for a foul occurs before the kick ends and a rekick is necessary, enforce the penalty and place the ball ready. If a kick goes out of bounds in your area, mark the out-of-bounds spot with a beanbag and throw your flag into the air if the receiving team did not touch it inbounds.

Also watch initial blocks by players near the receiving team's free-kick line and the action against the kicker and holder. Cover the action to the opposite 45-yard line. After the ball has gone downfield, move deliberately in that direction while watching for fouls away from the ball. You should maintain position to achieve coverage of the sideline at all times and be in position to take over coverage of the runner in your area on a long return.

### Covering Officials

The covering official or officials signal the clock to start when the kick is touched, other than the first touching by the kicker. For a kick out of bounds between the goal lines, sound the whistle, give the time-out signal, mark the spot and determine if the receiving team touched the ball inbounds. Toss a flag if the receiving team did not touch the ball.

As a covering official, you maintain position to cover the sideline at all times. When the ball becomes dead in your area, give the time-out signal. You should carry beanbags in your hands during the kickoff play.

## Field-Goal Attempt by Free Kick After Fair Catch

Although the play rarely occurs, a knowledgeable coach may try to pull off a field-goal attempt by a free kick after a fair catch or awarded fair catch. This situation presents a perfect example of the importance of knowing your duties, regardless of the situation.

### Referee

Take a position behind the uprights and work with the umpire to determine whether the kick is successful.

### Umpire

Take a position behind the uprights and rule on the crossbar, working with the referee to determine if the kick is successful.

### Other Officials

The other officials use the same mechanics that they use for the kick-off.

# Plays From Scrimmage

You will spend most of your time during a game officiating plays from scrimmage. Passing plays, running plays, punts, goal-line situations and field-goal attempts from various parts of the field are all examples of plays from scrimmage. Because these plays make up the bulk of the game, you should automatically know what to do in these situations. Reflex reactions result in smoothly run games.

## Reading Keys

If you knew what someone was going to say before he or she said it, you would be better prepared to react. The same is true about officiating football games. As an official you can anticipate, or better anticipate, a play before it begins by considering contextual cues and reading keys.

For instance, an offensive formation with two tight ends and no receivers is a cue to expect a running play. If a lineman's first move is forward, you know that a running play is underway—otherwise the lineman could be illegally downfield. If a tight end moved down the field without blocking, a passing play is probable. If a quarterback is in the shotgun formation and no back is in the backfield, watch for a pass. These are just a few examples of how considering contextual cues helps you anticipate the action, which in turn helps you be in the proper position.

Similarly, reading keys, or watching a specific player (or players) at the start of a play, can help determine coverage at the initial snap. You will still have to make adjustments after you read the keys given in figure 4.2 through 4.6 (pages 91-93), but knowing tendencies and players' positions will help you make the adjustments more quickly. You must be prepared to react to the play as it develops. Keys do not necessarily determine coverage for the entire play. Constant adjustments are necessary.

In five-person coverage, keys are most useful to the wing officials and back judge. The back judge has the first key, and the line judge and the linesman have the second key. All officials must remember not to key off the same player as another official. Do not key off the same player as the official ahead of you in the priority.

The back judge's assignment is based on the strength of the formation and the number of eligible receivers on one side of the ball. His normal assignment is the tight end on the strong side. Normally, one wing official keys off the receiver on the side where the strength is *not* declared, and the other wing official keys a strongside back.

When three receivers are on the same side (trips), the back judge works the two outside receivers and the wing official on that side works the inside eligible receiver. The wing official on the side where strength is *not* declared has primary key coverage over the end on his side. If a back is in motion, the strength may change by the location of the motion back at the snap.

In discussing and illustrating keys, several definitions are useful:

- *Strength of formation.* Determined by the number of eligible receivers on a particular side of the offensive formation. The designation of strength has nothing to do with the number of linemen on each side of the center; instead the number of eligible receivers outside the tackles determines the strength of the formation. If there is no strong side, strength is declared to the line judge's side (see figure 4.2, a-c).

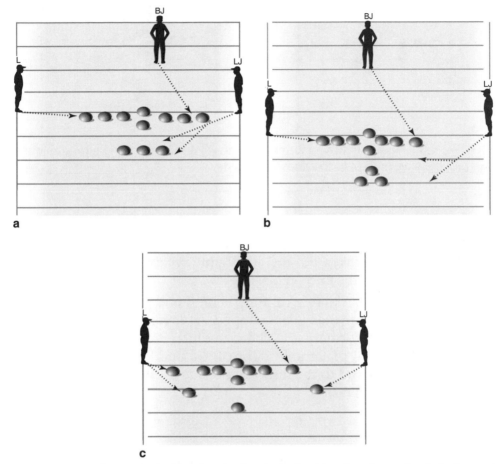

**FIGURE 4.2** Strength declared to the line judge's side when formation is balanced in (*a*) a T formation, (*b*) wishbone formation and (*c*) spread formation.

- *Tight end.* The end man on the line of scrimmage lined up no more than 4 yards from the nearest offensive lineman. Figure 4.3, a and b, illustrates double tight end formations where the back judge keys the tight end on the strong side while the wing official on that side keys the first back out of the backfield.
- *Back in backfield.* A player in the backfield between the tackles at the snap. Figure 4.3, a and b, illustrates a back causing strength to be declared to one side while figure 4.2c illustrates a balanced spread formation. When no strength is declared, the back judge keys the end on the line judge's side.

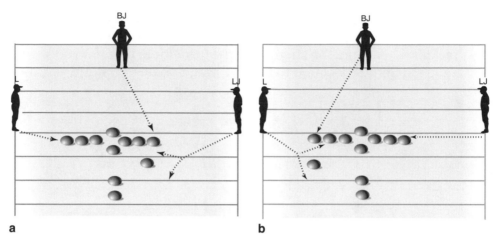

FIGURE 4.3   Double tight end formation with (*a*) a back showing strength to the line judge's side and (*b*) to the linesman's side.

- *Trips.* Three or more receivers outside one of the offensive tackles. In figure 4.4, the back judge keys the two outside receivers while the line judge takes the inside eligible receiver. The linesman is responsible for the end on his side.
- *Player in motion.* A player running behind and parallel to the line of scrimmage before the ball is snapped. A player in motion can cause the strength of formation to change, which requires the officials to key off different players. In figure 4.5, a and b, once the slot back has clearly moved to the line judge's side of the field, the strength is declared to that side.

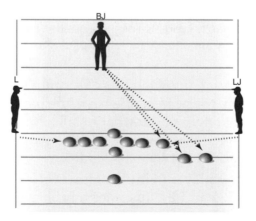

FIGURE 4.4   Trips to the line judge's side.

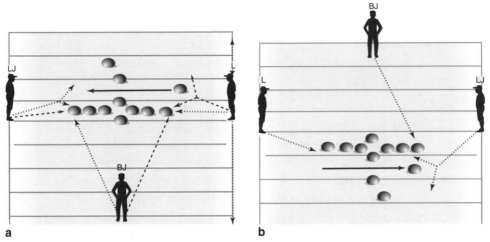

a                                                          b

FIGURE 4.5    *(a and b)* Motion in the backfield that changes strength of formation and keys.

## Running Plays

Running plays far outnumber passing plays in most high school football games. Some teams pass often, of course, but you should have a firm handle on how to react to running plays because they will be a major part of your responsibility when teams are lined up to run a play from scrimmage. Because you will spend much of your time officiating running plays, you must be thoroughly aware of your responsibilities (see figure 4.6).

Physical, tight, close-quarters action is often the norm on running plays. This kind of action is sometimes difficult to observe, but your scrutiny is required to ensure fair play and safety.

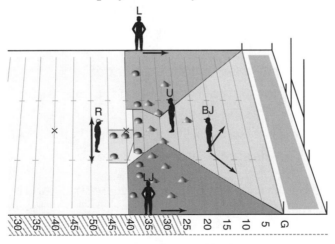

FIGURE 4.6    Starting positions and areas of responsibility on running and passing plays.

Knowing the following officials' responsibilities on running plays enhances both safe play and fairness. As in any other play, you should know the differences in responsibilities between a four- and five-person crew on a running play. Following are the mechanics for a five-person crew on a running play.

### Referee

After the ball is spotted, declare the ball ready for play by using the established procedure. As the referee, you take a position behind the offense. The distance back or to the side varies with the formation of the offense but is usually 3 to 4 yards deeper than the deepest back. You should stay on the passing-arm side of the quarterback and be able to view the tackle on the far side and the backs.

You should check the 25-second count and the 1-second count after a huddle or shift, count the number of offensive players (give a visible signal), eligible backs, snap irregularities and movement of linemen. You should also be alert for illegal shifts or players in motion.

After the snap, you have several areas of responsibility. Key the tackle on the opposite side. If he blocks aggressively, read the run. If he pass blocks, you should read the pass.

If the action is not in the direction of your original position, move toward or parallel to the scrimmage line, maintaining position approximately in line with the runner's progress. Delay moving immediately toward the line of scrimmage to avoid hindering a reverse or delayed play and to assure maximum vision of the play. Move behind the play toward the side of the field to which the play advances to cover the runner if he is downed near the line. You should check

- illegal use of hands by offensive players,
- action behind the ball and away from the runner near the neutral zone,
- action on the quarterback after the handoff,
- a signal from the linesman or line judge indicating the foremost point of the ball on quick line plays,
- backward or forward passes when the ball is thrown and
- the out-of-bounds spot behind the neutral zone.

Continue to observe the action behind the neutral zone before leaving the area. You are responsible for the runner until he crosses the neutral zone.

When the ball is dead, move quickly to its location and be positive of ball location before sounding the whistle. Signal the number of the next down and help spot the ball. Then give the ready-for-play signal and sound the whistle. At the end of the play, if the offensive team has made a first down or a change of team possession has occurred, give the time-out signal to stop the clock.

### Umpire

After the ball is spotted, remain over the ball until the referee gives the ready-for-play signal. As the umpire, you usually take a position 4 to 7 yards behind the defensive line and between the defensive ends, keeping the ball in view. Do not interfere with the vision or movement of the defensive backs. You should vary your position so that players cannot use you as interference.

You should also check

- the number of offensive players;
- the five players numbered 50 through 79 on the offensive line;
- interference with the snap, a false start or encroachment;
- disconcerting signals by the defense;
- the position of the ball between the inbounds lines and
- defensive players on the line of scrimmage in the free-blocking zone.

After the snap, you have several areas of responsibility. Key the center and guards. If they block aggressively, read the run. If they pass block, you should read the pass. You should also read the point of attack, paying particular attention to free-blocking zone restrictions.

When the play is wide to the side, move in that direction, observing the initial line play and action around the runner—especially on short gains or losses in side zones. Remain on the inside and work to the outside to maintain boxed-in coverage.

When a hole opens directly in front of you, react and adjust according to the play, moving laterally (with a quick step) from the hole and being alert for the tight end cutting across. Cover the action at the point of attack and then behind the runner. Check for illegal use of hands or arms and other fouls near the neutral zone. Be alert for a quick kick or pass, ineligible receivers down the field, the point where the forward pass first strikes anything, illegal contact on the snapper and action in and just behind the neutral zone. In addition, if a fumble occurs beyond the neutral zone, you should drop your beanbag and assist in determining who secures possession.

You should not sound the whistle unless the covering official is not in position to observe the spot where the ball becomes dead. Then spot the ball for the next down. You also assist with the relay if the ball goes out of bounds.

### Linesman and Line Judge

After the ball is spotted, as the linesman or line judge, you straddle the line the ball is on, no closer than 9 yards outside the widest offensive player, on the sideline if necessary. Check the down-marker number and signal the number of the down. Use an extended arm signal and hold it until the snap to indicate that the closest offensive player is off the line of scrimmage. Count the defensive players and identify eligible receivers on your side. Be alert for illegal substitutions.

You should observe the following:

- Wingbacks, flankers, split ends and slot backs
- The first two players in from your end of the offensive line, including backs, as eligible pass receivers
- A player in motion away from you, maintaining responsibility for him if he reverses direction
- A minimum of seven offensive players on the line of scrimmage
- Encroachment or a false start

After the snap, you have several areas of responsibility. For example, you are responsible for keying the end and the wide receiver if the defender is covering him tightly. If the end is uncovered, look through to the tackle to read the run or pass.

Be alert for quick plays into the line, assist in marking forward progress with your downfield foot, watch the initial charge of linemen and check blocks on eligible receivers. In addition, on an end run to the opposite side, you should observe the blocking near the neutral zone.

When the ball comes to your side of the field, cover the sideline and watch for crackback blocks. Sound the whistle when the ball becomes dead and move to the spot of the ball. If the ball becomes dead in a side zone, toss it to the referee or umpire for spotting. When the ball goes to the opposite side, move cautiously into that general area until you are certain that there will be no reverse or counter. Observe action on the linebacker and back-side pursuit. On down-the-line option plays toward you, observe the pitchman, a possible loose ball and the pitchman when he becomes the runner. Also, observe late blocks and fouls away from the runner.

The linesman and line judge are responsible for the entire sideline. If the ball goes out of bounds, signal time-out immediately and hold the out-of-bounds spot while another official retrieves the ball. While moving downfield with the runner, watch for an illegal forward pass or fumble. If play continues following an illegal forward pass, drop a penalty marker at the spot of the pass to indicate where the run ended.

When working with the line-to-gain equipment and crew, the linesman echoes the referee's signal orally and with the proper hand signal and repeats the referee's time-out signal. As the linesman, you should not turn your back on the field of play when you are having equipment moved for a first down. You also authorize the down-box operator to move only after the referee's signal.

When it is necessary to move the yardage chain, you should spot the foremost point of the ball with your downfield foot, have the down-box operator mark the spot, inform the referee that the yardage chain is ready and then move the chains off the sideline. When the line to gain is the goal line, fasten the clip to the chain at the intersection of the goal line and remove the line-to-gain equipment from the sideline.

### Back Judge

After the ball is spotted, take a position 15 to 20 yards beyond the defensive line of scrimmage, always deeper than the deepest defensive back. When the ball is on the inbounds line, you should be no wider than the near upright.

On single- or double-spread formations, adjust your position according to the location of the linesman and line judge to provide the best coverage. You should time the 25-second count and visibly count the last 5 seconds when on-field 25-second clocks are not used. Count the defensive players.

After the snap, you are responsible for the key tight end or the end on the strong side. If the formation is balanced, you should key on the end on the side of the line judge. On runs to either side of the field, move so that the runner is between you and either the linesman or the line judge while observing blocks in front of the runner. You should retreat to be in position behind the deepest receiver but should stay far enough away to keep the play boxed in while maintaining an inside-out coverage.

You should also cover players who are deeper than the linesman or line judge. When a runner breaks free, cover action around him and cover the goal line. On out-of-bounds runs, especially in team areas, move into the area of the dead ball and assist other officials in maintaining order.

### Covering Officials

As a covering official, you are responsible for keeping the play properly boxed in. Before sounding the whistle, be certain that the ball is dead, know the location of the ball and keep your eyes on the runner when you are covering.

When the ball becomes dead in your area, sound your whistle promptly and be alert for dead-ball fouls and surprise plays or fumbles. If a fumble occurs, mark the spot of the fumble with your beanbag and rule on possession immediately. If the defense recovers, immediately signal time-out and then signal first down. If the fumbling team recovers, the clock is not stopped. Indicate the number of the next down with your fingers, or your fist if it is fourth down. If the ball becomes dead before the fumble, sound the whistle immediately to indicate that the down has ended.

If the ball goes out of bounds, give the time-out signal immediately, mark and hold the spot, and continue to observe action. The nearest free official retrieves the ball, unless you (the covering official) are in the best position to do so. All other officials, excluding the covering official, echo the time-out signal and move quickly into position to assist in getting the ball ready for play. They should also be alert for substitution infractions.

## Forward Pass

A fifth official is helpful on running plays, but he becomes even more valuable on passing plays (see figure 4.6 on page 93 for starting positions and areas of responsibility on passing plays). Passing plays, as mentioned earlier, are usually less frequent than running plays in high school football. But that is only a general rule.

A team that has a quality passing game holds a distinct advantage. An official's lack of knowledge or inexperience in reacting to passing plays should not negate that edge. Following are the responsibilities of each person in a five-person crew on passing plays.

### Referee

After the ball is spotted, declare the ball ready for play by using the established procedure. As the referee, you position yourself on the passing-arm side of the quarterback and should be able to see the ball and the quarterback. Count offensive players, give the appropriate signal and identify eligible backs.

After the snap, read the block of the offensive tackle on the opposite side and observe all blocks behind the neutral zone. As the passer retreats, remain wide and deeper than the passer. You should give special attention to contact with the passer and continue to observe him, not the flight of the ball, after he releases it. Orally alert the defenders when the passer has released the ball, determine whether the pass is forward or backward and be alert for an illegal pass. When the pass is thrown from near the neutral zone, you then move to the spot of the pass to determine whether the passer's feet were in or behind the neutral zone when he released the ball. If the pass was illegal, drop a penalty marker and continue to officiate. If the pass was close, mark the spot of the pass with a beanbag and continue to officiate.

Additionally, you are solely responsible for intentional grounding, but may receive assistance from a covering official. Continue to observe the action behind the neutral zone before leaving the area. You are responsible for the runner until he crosses the neutral zone.

### Umpire

After the ball is spotted, remain over the ball until the referee gives the ready-for-play signal. As the umpire, you usually position yourself 4 to 7 yards behind the defensive line and between the defensive ends, keeping the snap in view. You should not interfere with the vision or movement of defensive backs and should vary your position so that players cannot use you for interference. Additionally, you should be sure to check

- the number of offensive players;
- the five players numbered 50 through 79 on the offensive line and ineligible receivers;
- interference with the snap, false starts or encroachment;
- disconcerting signals by the defensive team,
- the position of the ball between the inbounds lines and
- defensive players on the line of scrimmage in the free-blocking zone.

After the snap, be alert for illegal contact on the snapper and watch for illegal contact and illegal use of hands. When you read the forward pass, step toward the neutral zone to remove yourself as a target on shallow drag passes. This move also puts you in position to rule on whether an ineligible player is illegally downfield. You should also observe the action of players in and just behind the neutral zone, assist the referee in determining whether the passer's feet were in or behind the neutral zone when he released the ball and drop the penalty marker at the spot from which an illegal pass is thrown.

You also cover short passes down the middle and should know where the forward pass first touches. For a fumble in your area, mark the spot.

### Linesman and Line Judge

As the linesman, after the ball is spotted, check the down-box number and signal the number of the down to the referee. Position yourself just as you would for a running play, on the end of the line on the side of the line-to-gain equipment. Assist with the lineup.

As the line judge, you also have duties after the ball is spotted. Position yourself as you would for a running play, on the end of the line opposite the linesman. You should watch for illegal substitutions, count defensive players and identify eligible receivers. Use the extended-arm signal and hold it until the snap to indicate that the closest offensive player is off the line of scrimmage. Be alert for a player in motion away from you and maintain responsibility for the player if he reverses direction.

After the snap, both the linesman and line judge key through the end to read the initial block of the tackle and move to positions to check blocking and contact between eligible receivers and linebackers. Be ready to rule on the direction of a quick quarterback pass. Move cautiously downfield for 5 to 7 yards, approximately halfway between that zone and the deepest receiver, and watch for interference by either team.

Also be ready to rule on a fumble or illegal pass after a completion. If a pass is incomplete in the area of either official, sound the whistle, give the incomplete-pass signal, retrieve the ball and relay it to the official nearest the previous spot. Be ready to adjust coverage if a potential passer decides to run. Observe sideline action and forward progress of the runner. As either the linesman or line judge, you are responsible for the entire sideline but should always be prepared to come back to rule on a play near the neutral zone in addition to the sideline action.

### Back Judge

After the ball is spotted, take a position 15 to 20 yards beyond the defensive line of scrimmage and always deeper than the deepest defensive back. When the ball is on the inbounds line, position yourself no wider than the near upright. On single- or double-spread formations, adjust your position according to the location of the linesman and line judge to provide the best coverage. You are responsible for timing the 25-second count, visibly counting the last 5 seconds when on-field 25-second clocks are not used and for counting defensive players.

After the snap, key on the tight end as the play develops. Retreat to a position behind the deepest receivers and cover the deep receivers down the middle and to each sideline. When a pass is thrown, move quickly toward the ball and watch for interference by either team. Be ready to rule on a possible fumble or illegal pass after a completion and on all passes near the goal line and end line.

If a pass is incomplete in your area, sound the whistle, give the incomplete-pass signal, retrieve the ball and relay it to a nearby official. If a pass is complete, sound the whistle when the ball becomes dead and move to spot the ball. When the offensive team has reached the line to gain, give the time-out signal.

### Covering Officials

As a covering official, be alert for an illegal pass or touching or catching by an ineligible player both behind the neutral zone and beyond the neutral zone. Also watch for holding of eligible receivers and all contact beyond the neutral zone, both before and after the pass is thrown. If ruling on a pass reception involving the sideline, use the appropriate signal. If a player intercepts a pass inside the defensive team's 5-yard line and is downed in the end zone or the ball goes out of bounds, mark the spot of the interception with the beanbag and be prepared to rule whether the player's momentum took him into the end zone.

## Goal-Line Play

Plays from the goal line are similar, as far as officials' responsibilities go, to other plays from scrimmage, though positioning may vary slightly depending on where the snap is taken (see figures 4.7 and 4.8). The main differences occur in determining whether a team has scored and then performing the proper duties.

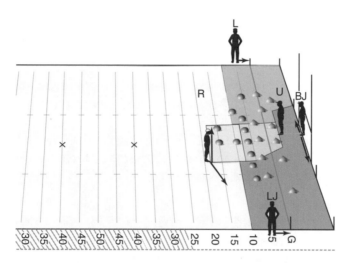

FIGURE 4.7   Starting positions and areas of responsibility near the goal line.

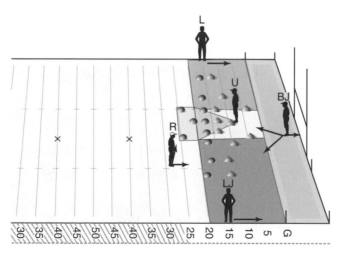

FIGURE 4.8   Starting positions and areas of responsibility for a ball snapped between the 10- and 20-yard lines.

Goal-line plays can be chaotic for players and coaches. Officials, however, should maintain their composure. Additional emotion or exaggerated signals are not necessary. Nothing eliminates credibility faster than an official who seems pleased or becomes emotional following a team's score or failure to score.

Officials on the goal line make subtle mechanical adjustments, but their demeanor should be the same as it is at midfield. Following are the mechanics of the goal-line situation for a five-person crew.

### Referee

As the referee, take the same position and cover the same way that you would for any scrimmage play. You should not give the touchdown signal from behind the runner until the linesman or line judge has signaled. Give the touchdown signal if another official has signaled it and no foul has occurred.

### Umpire

Take a position near the goal line and have the same coverage that you do for any scrimmage play. You should not give the touchdown signal from in front of the runner.

When a runner has made a quick thrust into the line, you should be sure that the ball is not moved forward after it is declared dead. You also assist the wing official if he needs help.

### Linesman and Line Judge

As the linesman or line judge on a goal-line play, take a position as you would for any scrimmage play. On a snap between the 10- and 5-yard lines, release slowly downfield and stay ahead of the runner to the goal line. Straddle the goal-line pylon while out of bounds. On a snap inside the 5-yard line, release to the goal line and officiate back to the ball. You should note the farthest point to which the ball is advanced by determining the following:

- If the ball is short of the goal line, move in quickly and help by marking the point with your downfield foot or by actually placing the ball.
- If the ball in the possession of the runner touches or crosses the goal-line plane, you should instantly give the touchdown signal.
- If the ball does not break the goal-line plane, you should not give the touchdown signal.

When working as the linesman with the line-to-gain crew, place the clip on the chain at the intersection with the goal line before removing it. Remove the line-to-gain equipment from the sideline when the line to gain is the goal line.

### Back Judge

As the back judge, do not take a position as deep as you would for other scrimmage plays. Start on the end line if the snap is on or inside the 10-yard line. You have complete responsibility for end-line coverage and time the 25-second count.

### All Officials

Only the official or officials who actually see the touchdown should give the touchdown signal. Officials who do not observe the touchdown should not mirror the signal. This procedure prevents confusion and eliminates the possibility that officials will give conflicting signals. More than one official may give the touchdown signal, but only if more than one saw the touchdown occur. A simple rule is this: If you do not see the ball cross the goal line, do not give the signal.

## Scrimmage Kicks

A fifth official is helpful in the punting game, mainly because officials must cover such a large part of the field. Scrimmage kicks are unique plays for officials because of the variety of situations that can arise, depending on the length of the kick, the side of the field the ball is kicked to, the length of the return or the possibility of a blocked kick. Crews should use the extra official to their advantage by following respective responsibilities and coverage zones (see figure 4.9).

A scrimmage kick combines the responsibilities of a play from scrimmage and a kick; two distinctly different activities occur during the same play. A smooth transition between the two is crucial, and executing can be difficult. If an official becomes bogged down with his scrimmage

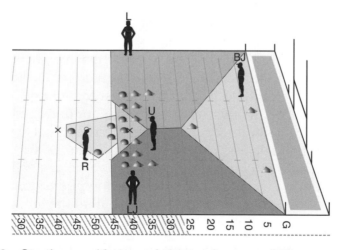

FIGURE 4.9   Starting positions and areas of responsibility on a scrimmage kick.

responsibilities, he will have difficulty taking care of the open-field action of a kick return. Likewise, if an official takes on kicking responsibilities too early, he will be unable to perform line-of-scrimmage duties properly. Following are the mechanics for a five-person crew in punting situations.

### Referee

After the ball is spotted, check the down and distance with the linesman and declare the ball ready for play by using the established procedure. Take a position 3 to 4 yards in advance of and 5 to 7 yards outside the player in the kicker's position, on the kicking-leg side. You should count the kicking team's players.

After the snap, watch for fouls behind the neutral zone, especially near the kicker. You also are alert for a blocked kick and are ready to rule on a recovery. After the ball crosses the neutral zone, observe line play and move downfield slowly, following the kick. Watch for fouls and be ready to pick up the runner if he breaks a long return. Determine from the covering official if the ball was touched beyond the neutral zone and by whom.

For a kick out of bounds in flight, you have several responsibilities. If the kick is long, move to the spot where the kicker kicked the ball then line up the covering official with the spot where the ball crossed the sideline by using an outstretched arm. If the kick is short, go directly to the out-of-bounds spot. If no foul occurs, signal the linesman to move the line-to-gain equipment. Obtain the ready sign from the linesman before giving the ready-for-play signal.

### Umpire

After the ball is spotted, take a position 4 to 7 yards deep, keeping the snap in view. Count the punting team's players and check numbering exceptions. Key on the offensive guards and center.

After the snap, step toward the neutral zone and be alert for roughing the snapper. Then shift to the action of the offensive guards and backs behind the neutral zone. Read the play and be alert for a fake punt, either a run or a pass. You should be ready to assist the referee in covering a short or blocked kick. You also are responsible for determining whether the ball crosses the neutral zone. Following the kick, pivot to view the line judge's side of the field and observe any blocks in the side zone. Move toward the return area, observing players away from the ball. You should be alert for fouls in the secondary and move downfield slowly. If the ball goes out of bounds, move to help relay the ball to the inbounds spot.

### Linesman and Line Judge

After the ball is spotted, take the same position as you do for a run or pass, check the down number and count the receiving team's players.

As the linesman after the snap, hold momentarily to see whether the ball crosses the neutral zone. Then move slowly downfield, covering your side between the neutral zone and the deep receiver or receivers. As the line judge, release on the snap and move downfield, covering your side between the neutral zone and the deep receiver or receivers. Both the linesman and line judge cover all kicks to their respective sides.

As either the linesman or line judge, if the ball goes out of bounds in flight on your side, sound the whistle and give the time-out signal. The official on the side where the ball went out of bounds moves farther downfield than where it went out and walks upfield until the referee spots him on the sideline. If the ball rolls out of bounds, sound the whistle, give the time-out signal, hold the spot and continue to observe the action. The official drops his beanbag at the spot if the ball must be retrieved.

The linesman and line judge assist the referee in covering the ball on a short or blocked kick. Note whether the kick is touched beyond the neutral zone or recovered in or behind the neutral zone. Also be prepared to mark a first touching, a fumble or the end of the kick.

For a routine kick, unless the kick comes close to your side, delay your move to the sideline and cover clipping and other fouls in the secondary. Move with the runner if the runner comes to your side, and follow him to the goal line if the run is broken. When the ball becomes dead, sound your whistle, give the time-out signal, mark the spot and make sure of possession on a fair catch.

As the line judge, you should also observe the action of a signaler when no fair catch is made. If you call a foul, another official covers the ball while you report the information to the referee. As the linesman, watch the referee for the signal to move the line-to-gain equipment.

### Back Judge

After the ball is spotted, take a position 7 to 10 yards wider than and in front of the deepest receiver on the linesman's side of the field. Count the receiving team's players.

After the snap, carry your beanbag in your hand during the down to mark the first touching, momentum, fumble or the end of the kick. When the kick is short to either sideline, the linesman or line judge assumes responsibility for the ball and you observe the action of players around the ball. You cover a long or deep kick out of bounds on the linesman's side.

If the kicked ball goes out in flight, sound the whistle and give the time-out signal. The referee should spot you on the sideline. Hold the spot until the ball is placed on the ground. Cover all kicks down the middle and be ready to rule on whether either team touches the kick. If the ball is muffed, be prepared to rule on possession. Be alert for a handoff or reverse. When the kicking team is first to touch a punt that is moving, mark the spot of the first touching with your beanbag and continue to cover the play. If the kicking team is first to touch the kick at rest beyond the neutral zone, sound the whistle, give the time-out signal and mark the spot.

After a fair catch, sound the whistle, give the time-out signal and mark the spot. Be sure that the referee knows that a fair catch was made. When a fair catch is not made, stay with the ball and let the line judge observe the action by the signaler. Move with the runner who catches the kick and advances. Other officials will ordinarily pick up the runner near the line of scrimmage. When they do, delay and observe the action behind the ball. When one of the other officials is screened out and not able to pick up the runner, move with the runner and sound the whistle when the ball becomes dead.

When the kick becomes dead, sound the whistle immediately and give the time-out signal. Be prepared to rule on a touchback while giving appropriate signals and inform the referee of ball status before placing it for the next play. If a player catches the kick inside the 5-yard line and is downed in his end zone or if the ball goes out of bounds there, be prepared to rule on whether the player's momentum took him into the end zone. Mark the spot of a catch inside the 5-yard line with a beanbag.

# Field-Goal Attempts

Unlike in a four-person crew, in which officials' responsibilities change depending on whether the snap for the field-goal attempt is from inside or outside the 15-yard line, the responsibilities of a five-person crew (see figure 4.10) are the same no matter where the field-goal attempt occurs.

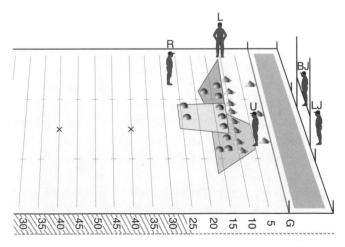

FIGURE 4.10   Starting positions and areas of responsibility on a field-goal attempt.

Like a punt, a field-goal attempt is a hybrid between a play from scrimmage and the kicking game. Although returns do not normally occur, they are within the rules and happen occasionally in high school football—particularly on long field-goal attempts. So stay alert if the attempt is particularly short and in the field of play. Following are the guidelines for a five-person crew's responsibilities from all distances.

### Referee

After the ball is spotted, take a position about 1 yard to the rear and at least 2 to 3 yards to the side of the potential kicker at about a 45-degree angle. Be sure that you are able to see the face of the holder and able to see him receive the ball. Count the kicking team's players and observe the kicker, holder and opposite-side tackle.

After the snap, watch for a fumble by the holder and cover as usual if a run or pass occurs. You also assist in sideline coverage if a run develops to the vacated line-judge side. Signal score or no score after receiving a signal from the line judge or back judge, and rule on roughing the kicker or holder. If a try is blocked, immediately sound your whistle and give the no-score signal. If a field-goal attempt is blocked, the ball remains live.

### Umpire

After the ball is spotted, position yourself 4 to 7 yards deep, keeping the ball in view. Check for use of numbering exceptions. Key on the action of the center and guards.

After the snap, step toward the neutral zone, reading the interior linemen, checking the action on the snapper, whether a kick crosses the neutral zone and short or blocked kicks.

Also be ready to assist the referee in covering a short or blocked kick, and be alert for action on or by the outside offensive linemen and the up blocking back on the vacated line-judge side. Shift observation to the contact between defensive players and blockers behind the line. After players go past your position, pivot to view the line judge's side of the field, observe blocks in the side zone and move toward the play to observe the action. Assist in goal-line coverage if a run develops to the vacated line-judge side.

### Linesman

After the ball is spotted, take a position 5 to 7 yards outside the offensive end and observe the neutral zone.

After the snap, if a pass or run develops, move with the play as you do on any other goal-line play. Then quickly move to the goal-line pylon if a run develops to the line-judge side.

### Line Judge and Back Judge

After the ball is spotted, the line judge and back judge take positions beyond the end zone, each behind an assigned upright. Position behind your upright where you feel most comfortable and have the best coverage. Count the defensive team's players. As the back judge, you're responsible for timing the 25-second count. The line judge and back judge tell each other the numbers of the eligible receivers.

After the snap, assume responsibility for the end line and for determining whether the kick goes over or under the crossbar and inside the uprights. As the back judge, you rule on the crossbar and upright. As the line judge, you rule only on the upright. As the back judge, sound the whistle when a successful kick passes the uprights or when the kick is apparently unsuccessful after breaking the goal-line plane. Signal score or no score and be prepared to move if the kick is blocked, obviously short or a fake. Then key on the tight end on your side. If a run develops to the vacated side, if you're the line judge, move quickly along the end line to the back pylon to rule on the sideline. The next move is toward the goal line to assist. When run situations develop to your side, you have primary sideline responsibility with assistance from the referee. Be ready to mark first touching, a fumble, momentum or the end of the kick.

### All Officials

Take positions for a field goal or attempt if the kicking tee is brought onto the field. Also be alert for a runback of an unsuccessful field-goal attempt that is caught or recovered in the field of play.

# After Touchbacks, Safeties, Tries and Field-Goal Attempts

The mechanics and responsibilities for officials are identical after touchbacks, safeties, tries and field-goal attempts. Officials' positions will be slightly different, depending on which play they are covering, but responsibilities will be the same after all three plays. Following are the mechanics for a five-person crew.

### Referee

The referee declares the ball ready for play by using established procedure. He counts the team's players and should be alert for illegal substitutions.

### Umpire

Be alert for substitutions and any irregularities in the number of players on the defensive or receiving team. Move to your proper position and count the proper team's players.

### Linesman

Take the ball to the center of the field on the proper yard line and place it with the foremost point on the center of the line. Count the team's players and be alert for substitutions. Hand the ball to the kicker if it is to be put in play by a free kick, and instruct the kicker to wait for the referee's signal. Then move to the sideline where the line-to-gain equipment is located.

### Line Judge

Retrieve any kicked ball. If a kickoff is to follow, the down-box operator should retrieve the ball and relay it to you, who will in turn relay it to the linesman. Then count players on the proper team. Also be alert for substitutions.

### Back Judge

Count the proper team's players and time the 25-second count when appropriate. Be alert for illegal substitutions.

### All Officials

Be alert for substitutions and any irregularities in the number of players. Do not permit any team attendants on the field following a touchback. You should strive to put the ball in play immediately.

Remember, for a free kick following a safety, each official assumes the same relative position and has the same duties as on kickoffs, except the kicking team's free-kick line becomes the 20-yard line instead of the 40-yard line (see figure 4.11). The kicking team can put the ball in play by a punt, place kick or drop kick.

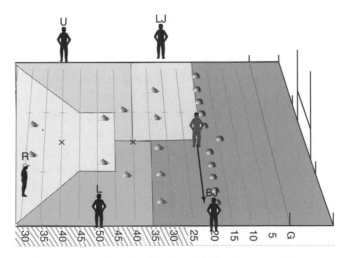

FIGURE 4.11    Starting positions on a free kick after a safety.

# Administrative Duties

Officials should not consider these administrative tasks "extra" duties or "throw-in" responsibilities. Your quick reaction when performing administrative duties such as enforcing penalties, making first-down measurements, calling time-outs and ending periods is essential to keeping the game moving.

Delays should not occur when these situations arise in a football game. An official who knows what to do and when to do it can keep things moving along. Maintaining the flow of the game instills confidence that you are in control of the game—every facet of the game. Following are the administrative duties of a five-person crew.

## Enforcing the Rules

Nothing in a football game is more annoying than having an official or an officiating crew take over the action. New officials, who sometimes consider throwing the flag their primary duty, often make this mistake. Certainly, enforcing the rules and administering penalties is important. But just as important is understanding that you are not to be the center of the game. Your job is to enforce the rules, enhance safety and keep the game flowing.

When fouls occur, simply call the infractions and enforce the rules but don't become the star of the show. Stay professional and unemotional. If a rule is broken, take action and continue. Following are the mechanics of administering penalties in a five-man crew.

### Referee

When the ball is dead after a foul, as the referee, give the time-out signal, obtain full information from the official who called the foul, give a preliminary signal to the press-box side of the field only and give options to the captain of the offended team.

When a captain's most advantageous choice is obvious, quickly inform him of the options. If the captain does not respond, consider his silence acceptance of the obvious choice. Once he makes a choice, he cannot revoke it. Make note of the enforcement spot for the penalty and confirm the yardage with the umpire. After the ball has been spotted, give the final signal for the foul to the press-box side of the field only.

When a penalty is declined, go to the spot of the ball and give the press box the foul signal followed by the penalty-declined signal. When a double foul occurs, signal each foul, facing the press box, and then give the penalty-declined signal. When enforcing two penalties, give proper signals following each enforcement. When the penalty is to be enforced on the kickoff, indicate the scoring signal, follow with the proper foul signal, point to the offending team and point toward the succeeding spot. After an accepted penalty for a foul by either team during the last timed down of a period, play continues with an untimed down.

### Umpire

As the umpire, secure the ball, make a note of the enforcement spot for the penalty and proceed with measurement. On a properly marked field, you should avoid stepping off the distance between yard lines, except to the first yard line and for the final yard line. Walk briskly, using an arm signal to point to each yard line you cross.

### Linesman

Be certain of the down number and go to the succeeding spot. Be ready to have the line-to-gain equipment moved if penalty administration results in a first down.

You will also check enforcement. Do not permit trainers, attendants or coaches to come onto the field. Relay penalty information to the appropriate coach and to other officials if necessary.

### Line Judge

Return the time-out signal to the referee and hold the enforcement spot. As the line judge, you also check enforcement. Do not permit trainers, attendants or coaches to come onto the field. Relay penalty information to the appropriate coach and to other officials if necessary.

### Back Judge

As the back judge, you help obtain the ball and assist in holding the spot of the foul or recovering the penalty marker. You also assist in relaying foul information to the appropriate sideline. Give the final signal for the foul to be enforced on a kickoff to the press-box side of the field.

### All Officials

When observing a live-ball foul, withhold the whistle. Drop a penalty marker at the proper yard line and continue to observe play, noting the location of the ball at the time of the foul. When the ball becomes dead, give the time-out signal, sound the whistle and orally report the information to the referee in the presence of the umpire. Give no visible signal and make a mental note about whether the clock should be started on ready or on the snap.

If you observe a dead-ball foul, sound your whistle, toss a penalty marker into the air and give the time-out signal immediately. Then report the information orally to the referee and see that the umpire assesses the penalty properly in all respects.

After calling the foul and after the ball has been declared dead, the calling official (umpire, linesman, line judge or back judge) sounds a whistle and stops the clock. Get the referee's attention by giving short blasts of the whistle. Make sure that another official is covering the flag at the spot of the foul and orally report full information to the referee by

- identifying the foul;
- identifying the offending team including jersey color and offense or defense, or kicking or receiving team;
- identifying the offending player's number or position;
- indicating the spot of the foul, end of the run or end of the kick and
- indicating the status of the ball when the foul occurred.

Assist with locating the captains and recovering penalty markers and the ball.

For enforcement, as a calling official, stay clear of the spot of the foul. If the spot is different, then go to the enforcement spot. When the umpire begins enforcement, check for correctness and distance. Avoid visiting while the penalty is assessed. When you call a disqualifying foul, inform the offending player and report his number and the type of infraction to the referee, coach and other members of the officiating crew. Emphasize that disqualification is for the remainder of the game. If double disqualifying fouls occur, the referee may designate another official to assist in reporting the fouls to coaches. As the official, you shall not place a hand on the offending player or accompany or escort him to the sideline.

All officials should record the player's number and name, if known, and observe all other players. After the contest, the referee should notify the state association if applicable and report unsportsmanlike penalties.

## First-Down Measurements

As in any other facet of the game, officials have distinct positions and responsibilities when measuring for first downs using the traditional rods and chain (see figure 4.12). If another method of measurement is being used, officials must be aware of that before the game begins. Officials should be familiar with the method being used. If they haven't used it before, talking over the procedures with the line-to-gain crew would be prudent.

Officials should stress to the "chain gang" the importance of getting on and off the field quickly. Nothing slows a game more than confusion or uncertainty on every measurement, regardless of the number of officials in a crew. Following are the mechanics of first-down measurements when working in a five-person crew.

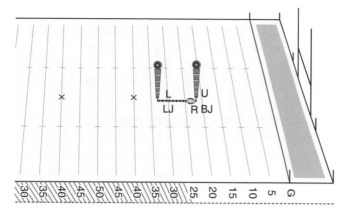

FIGURE 4.12   Officials' positions on a first-down measurement.

### Referee

As the referee, you give the time-out signal and signal the linesman to bring the chain onto the field. Motion players away from the ball. Rotate the ball so that the long axis is parallel to the sideline (see figure 3.11c on page 79 of chapter 3). In a side zone, measure before the ball is taken to the inbounds line. If the line to gain is not reached in the side zone, use the chain to place the ball accurately at the inbounds spot.

If the ball has gone out of bounds, measure to the point where the ball crossed the sideline. The inside edge of the forward rod marks the line to gain. When measurement is complete, signal the number of the next down, spot the ball at the proper place and wait for the line-to-gain crew to return to position. If a new series is awarded to the opponent of the team that was in possession when the ball became dead, place the chains so that the foremost point of the ball when it became dead becomes the rear point for the new direction. Set the new rear rod with the inside edge at the new point of the ball so that the line to gain is 10 yards in advance of that point.

After measurement, obtain ready signs from the captains and declare the ball ready for play by using established procedure. If the ball was not out of bounds, signal the clock to start with your declaration of ready for play. If the ball turns over on downs, start the clock on the snap.

### Umpire

Take the forward rod from the chainman at the place of measurement. When the linesman says, "Ready," tighten the chain and hold the forward rod near the ball until the referee reaches a decision.

### Linesman

When the referee signals for a measurement, grasp the chain and clip at the back edge of the back yard line (not just grasping the clip because it could detach). Instruct the down-box operator to mark the front rod spot and keep the same down number. Then take the chain behind the ball and place the clipped part of the chain at the back edge of the back yard line. Hold it firmly and call, "Ready" to the umpire to stretch the chain tight and wait for the referee's decision and signal.

If the location of the ball does not result in a first down, you (while holding the chain) accompany the crew to the sideline and reset it in the original position. Have the down-box operator move the indicator to the next down. If the location of the ball results in a new series, set the inside edge of the rear rod at the foremost point of the ball after the referee spots it. First down should be on the marker. Mark the foremost point of the ball for the down-marker operator on all first downs.

### Line Judge

Position yourself behind the yard line from which the measurement will be made and align the linesman with the ball so that the measurement is accurate.

### Back Judge

You should not permit team attendants to enter the field. Help clear players from the measurement area, observe all players and tend the ball at the time of measurement.

## Conventional Time-Outs

Officials should be able to recognize quickly when a team or head coach is calling a time-out. Promptness here is vital, as is a good, crisp signal to the game clock. To help make this happen, officials must stay cognizant of the game situation. By knowing when a time-out is likely, they will be able to call it quickly and effectively. Officials must be alert! Proper, timely time-out calls can sometimes make a difference in the outcome of a game. Officials should strive never to allow a sloppy time-out call or lack of knowledge of the game situation to affect the game. Following are the officials' responsibilities during time-outs when working in a five-person crew.

### Referee

When a time-out occurs, sound the whistle and signal time-out. If the time-out is charged to a team, indicate so by moving both arms three times in a horizontal motion toward that team. Indicate an official's time-out by tapping your chest with both hands.

As referee, your duties during a time-out are to

- check the number of time-outs remaining for each team,
- check the time remaining with the back judge,

- check the down with the linesman and
- notify the coach and captain after a third time-out has been charged.

Then take a position away from the other officials and observe the defense. When the back judge notifies you that 45 seconds have expired, signal the linesman and line judge by pointing directly at them to give their teams the 15-second warning. Inform each team huddle, notifying the defensive team first, of the down and time remaining in the period. Declare the ball ready for play by using established procedure.

### Umpire
During a time-out, maintain a position over the ball and observe the offense until the referee is ready to start play.

### Linesman and Line Judge
During a time-out, both the linesman and line judge move to positions halfway between the ball and the sideline. Be alert for the signal from the referee to give your respective team the 15-second warning. Go to the team huddle and say, "Coach, the ball will be ready for play in 15 seconds." Be alert for substitutions by the team on your sideline or if a team attempts to use substitutes for the purpose of deception. Maintain the proper number of players and attendants in the huddle when conferences are held between the inbounds lines.

### Back Judge
During a time-out, time the 60-second interval and notify the referee at 45 seconds and again when the 60-second interval expires.

### All Officials
Repeat the time-out signal and record the time-out, the number of the player who called it, the time on the clock and the period. You should stand alertly erect and not visit with players. Discussion should be restricted to captains only. Do not huddle with other officials in a group.

## Injury Time-Outs

The following section describes additional responsibilities for a five-person crew beyond regular time-out duties when an injury occurs. As you might expect, handling an injury situation is important. Someone is hurt. Quick action is imperative. Panic, however, shouldn't be part of the equation.

### Referee
Summon the trainer or trainers and coaches on the field and determine whether the injured player is or was unconscious. If so, inform the coach

that the player may not return to the game without written approval from a physician. Be ready to assist the trainer or trainers and coaches in securing additional medical help, if needed. Attempt to keep players a significant distance away from the seriously injured player or players by directing players and coaches toward their respective team-bench areas.

After the medical staff begins to work on an injured player, all members of the officiating crew should control the total playing-field environment and team personnel and allow the medical staff to perform services without interruption or interference. Officials should ensure adequate lines of vision between the medical staff and all available emergency personnel. The officiating crew should control players and coaches so that they do not influence medical services performed by the athletic trainers or team physicians or complain about the time taken to perform such services.

### Umpire
Make sure that the summoned trainers or coaches are not on the field for coaching purposes.

## End-of-Period Procedure

The end-of-period action is simple, especially when field clocks are clearly visible. Officials should be aware when time is running out and make sure that no play begins after the clock ticks to zero. With five officials, the back judge comes into play on the end-of-play procedure, which differs significantly from the procedure used by a four-person crew. Following are the end-of-period procedures for a five-person crew.

### Referee
If a field clock is not used, take an official's time-out with approximately four minutes remaining in the second and fourth periods, inform both captains of the time remaining and see that both coaches are notified. When time expires and the ball becomes dead, sound the whistle and repeat the time-out signal.

If a field clock is used, when facing the clock, you are responsible for knowing when time expires. If time expires before a snap, sound your whistle to prevent the snap, if possible. If the ball is snapped immediately after time expires, sound your whistle loud and long and give the time-out signal. After a delay to ensure that no foul, no obvious timing error, no request for a coach-referee conference or no other irregularity has occurred, hold the ball in one hand over your head to signal the official end of the period.

### Back Judge
If a field clock is not used, notify the referee approximately four minutes before the end of the second and fourth periods. Approximately

30 seconds before time for the period expires, notify the referee that time may expire during the next down. When time expires and the ball becomes dead, signal the referee by raising an arm above your head, sounding your whistle and giving the time-out signal.

If a field clock is used, when facing the clock, you are responsible for knowing when time expires. If time expires before the snap, sound your whistle to prevent the snap, if possible. If the ball is snapped immediately after time expires, sound your whistle loud and long and give the time-out signal.

## Between Periods

The time between periods involves a basic procedure that officials can make simple with a little understanding and communication. Both teams and the officials should have a clear understanding of what the procedures are between periods, including how much time there will be between periods. These items should be cleared up before the ending of the period. Officials should stay organized and professional even between periods. Following are the duties for a five-person crew.

### Referee

As referee, you note and record the down, distance and yard line nearest the foremost point of the ball. Announce this information to the other officials and confirm it with the linesman and umpire. You measure the distance from the nearest yard line to the foremost point of the ball and estimate the distance from the inbounds line. In spotting the ball at the other end of the field, check again with the linesman and umpire.

When the back judge notifies you that 45 seconds have expired, signal the linesman and line judge to give their teams the 15-second warning. When the back judge notifies you that 60 seconds have expired, announce the down and distance from near the ball. Declare the ball ready for play by using established procedure.

### Umpire

Record the down, distance and yard line nearest the foremost point of the ball and assist the referee. Quickly take the ball to the corresponding point on the other half of the field and reverse the direction.

### Linesman

Record the down, distance and yard line nearest the foremost point of the ball. Confirm the information with the referee and grasp the chain and the clip, which is near the back stake. Note that the clip should have been attached to the chain at the beginning of the series of downs. Also call the down and distance to your assistants, reverse ends of the yardage chain and set the yardage chain after the referee spots the ball. Check the number of the down and distance to gain. Indicate to the referee that you're ready by signaling the number of the down with your fingers, or your fist for fourth down.

### Line Judge and Back Judge

Observe the teams while moving to the corresponding spot on the other end of the field and assume the same responsibilities that you would for a time-out. Check the team box and huddle areas for appropriate conference procedure, as you do during a charged time-out.

As the back judge, you time the 60-second interval and notify the referee at 45 seconds and again when the 60-second interval expires. As the line judge, you give your team a 15-second warning when the referee directs you to do so.

### All Officials

Between periods, no more than three team attendants are permitted on the field between the inbounds lines. Either legal type of coach-player conferences may be held.

## Between Halves

The duties that officials perform at halftime are similar to those they perform between periods. A few differences are notable. Communication becomes even more important because at halftime teams usually gather away from the field and the officials. But as long as all parties are aware of the halftime procedures long before halftime, there shouldn't be a problem. Following are the duties of a five-person crew.

### Referee

Between halves, instruct the time operator to time the intermission. At the end of the intermission, you are responsible for ensuring that three minutes is placed on the clock for the mandatory warm-up period before the start of the second half after the intermission time elapses. Signal the time operator when to start the clock to time intermission. Additionally, give the game ball to the linesman.

As referee, you should avoid visiting with anyone. Discuss situations only in the dressing room or other private place. You determine which team has the choice for the second half. Escort the captain to the center of the field and relay the choices to the team bench and press box with appropriate signals.

### Umpire

For the captains' meeting before the second half, escort the captain to the center of the field and move to the sideline near the 20-yard line opposite the linesman.

### Linesman

During the intermission, discuss with the line-to-gain crew any aspects of their duties that they might improve to aid in game administration.

In preparing for the second half, station the line-to-gain crew near the team box and on the receiving team's end of the field, then take a position at the sideline on the 30-yard line.

### Line Judge and Back Judge

As line judge, take a position near the sideline on the receiving team's free-kick line; as the back judge, keep time during intermission and take a position near the sideline on the kicking team's free-kick line opposite the linesman.

### All Officials

All officials should leave the field together and assemble in the dressing room or other private place. Discuss the overtime procedure if applicable. Return to the field at least five minutes before the second half is to begin. Be sure to start the second half on time.

# PART III

# APPLYING THE RULES

# CHAPTER 5

# THE GAME

Now you get to have a little fun. So far, we've presented technical information—important information—but in chapters 5, 6 and 7 of this book, we are going to bring some situations to life for you, action that you might actually face during a game. Then we leave it up to you to decide what ruling to make. We will present scenarios dealing with a series of rules, and then at the end of the chapter, we will give you the ruling you should have made.

In this chapter, we'll consider cases in the first four rules:

- Rule 1: Players, Field and Equipment
- Rule 2: Definitions of Playing Terms
- Rule 3: Periods, Time Factors and Substitutions
- Rule 4: Ball in Play, Dead Ball and Out of Bounds

## Rule 1: Players, Field and Equipment

Rule 1 details the physical items you see when you look at a football game: the players, the field and the equipment. The Rule 1 cases we quiz you on include number of players, teams entering the field, choice of ball, legal and illegal equipment and video replays. Consider how you'd respond in each situation and check your judgments against the answers beginning on page 129 at the end of the chapter.

### CASE 1: Number of Players

The Broncos and the Mustangs have been involved in an extremely emotional game during which several skirmishes have broken out, but up until now they have been kept under control. That is about to change.

With time ticking away, the Broncos have the ball and a slim lead, so they decide to run out the clock. The Mustangs, who are the home team, have no time-outs left and now realize that they are about to be beaten in front of their fans by a heated rival. Some of the Mustangs players decide to exact revenge.

The Broncos quarterback takes a knee with about two minutes to go. That's when things get ugly. A couple of Mustangs take a cheap shot at the quarterback, some Broncos teammates come to his defense, and before you know it a melee erupts.

Before order is restored, several players from each team are ejected from the game, including some from the bench. When the officials sort things out to play the last couple of minutes of the game, they discover that the Broncos have 11 players available to play and the Mustangs have only 9. No other players are available because of the mass disqualifications.

Can the game continue even though the Mustangs don't have 11 players? What is your ruling?

### CASE 2: Teams Entering the Field

The Cougars are playing their homecoming game against their cross-town rivals, the Chargers. All the pregame festivities have ended, and now the teams—more accurately, the coaches—decide it's time for some pregame head games.

Neither team wants to go onto the field. The Cougars, with the bleachers packed with homecoming fans, want the Chargers to enter the field first. And the Chargers, not wanting to allow the Cougars the opportunity for one last huge cheer just before game time, decide to wait out their hosts. So both teams just stand there, not budging. Obviously, one of the teams must take the field. Yet, just as clearly, neither of them is about to take the field until the officials force them to make a move.

Who must go on the field first? The visiting Chargers or the home-standing Cougars?

What is your ruling?

### CASE 3: Choice of Ball

"Ball Day" is ordinarily considered a special day at a baseball game; the first 10,000 fans to enter the stadium receive a baseball. But in a high school football game you are officiating between the Panthers and the Bulldogs, you think you've got your own version of "Ball Day" going on.

On four occasions, you find yourself in a situation in which one team or the other makes a request to change balls. Here are the requests:

1. The Panthers request that a rubber ball be put in play on second down after they used a leather ball on first down.
2. The Panthers, under dry conditions, request that a different leather ball be put in play on fourth down after using another leather ball for the previous plays of the series.
3. The Panthers score a touchdown with a leather ball and request that a different leather ball be put in play for the point-after-touchdown try.

A change of ball request should only be granted under certain circumstances.

4. The Bulldogs recover the kickoff and request that a new ball be put in play.

In each situation, what is your ruling?

### CASE 4: Legal and Illegal Equipment

Just before game time, a coach approaches you and says, "Hey, ref, my cornerback's got an arm injury, but he's wearing this protective splint. Just letting you know."

You examine the splint, or cast, on the forearm of the cornerback and notice that it is made of a hard material and is covered with at least a half inch of high-density, closed-cell polyurethane. As you examine the splint, the coach pulls out a document from a licensed physician stating that the protective device is necessary to prevent injury.

The coach wants to know if his cornerback can wear the device. What is your ruling?

### CASE 5: Video Replays

The Razorbacks fullback pounds into the interior of the line from the Tigers' 2-yard line. A stack of players piles up at the goal line, and the officials signal a touchdown. Replay equipment clearly shows that the Razorbacks fullback never crossed the goal line. The Tigers see the tape and want to show it to you. What is your ruling?

# Rule 2: Definitions of Playing Terms

Rule 2 lists definitions of some playing terms and the correct interpretation of those terms. The Rule 2 cases we quiz you on include blocking, catching, calling a conference and passing or fumbling. Decide how you would rule and then check your answers beginning on page 130 at the end of the chapter.

### CASE 6: Legal and Illegal Blocking

The Bears have the ball, it is third and 19, and their quarterback goes back to pass. The Bears right tackle makes a block on the Blazers defensive tackle, making legal contact on the defensive tackle's chest using extended arms with open hands. The defensive tackle spins to try to reach the quarterback. The offensive tackle effectively maintains contact with the defender, shifting his hands to the defender's upper arm and then directly on his back as the defender turns.

The Bears quarterback is safe because his offensive tackle continues the block on the defender and forces him beyond the quarterback. At any point in this block, was a violation committed? What is your ruling?

### CASE 7: Catching the Ball

The Pirates' passing game has been clicking all night, and this play is no exception. The quarterback throws a perfect spiral to a receiver who leaps high in the end zone to make the catch. The receiver briefly has possession, but the Lancers safety drills him before the receiver comes down to the ground. The ball is knocked loose right into the hands of another Pirates receiver in the end zone.

The Pirates "second" receiver is inbounds. He possesses the ball and begins celebrating an apparent touchdown. But is it a touchdown? What is your ruling?

### CASE 8: Conference

On an unseasonably hot and humid early autumn night in Michigan, the Trojans and the Shamrocks have been struggling with the heat. You have the authority to call an official's time-out for heat and humidity, and you do so.

During the time-out, the Shamrocks hold a conference in the middle of the field. All 11 players are involved, and the Shamrocks head coach, wearing a headset, enters the conference. During the conference, the head coach talks to an assistant on the sideline with the headset. Is it a legal conference? What is your ruling?

### CASE 9: Pass or Fumble

A quarterback has been under heavy pressure all night, but his team is down and he continues to try to get the passing game going. The quarterback drops back, and this time the rush gets to him. He is hit hard while in the throwing motion. When he was hit and lost possession, the quarterback's arm was extended back but not moving in either direction.

The ball squirts loose and a defensive end pounces on it for an apparent fumble recovery. Is the exuberant defender's celebration justified? Is it a fumble or an incomplete pass? What is your ruling?

# Rule 3: Periods, Time Factors and Substitutions

Rule 3 covers periods, time factors and substitutions, outlining the protocol for each. The Rule 3 cases we quiz you on include resolving tied games, halftime intermissions, starting and stopping the clock and substitutions.

### CASE 10: Resolving Tied Games

The Bucs and the Lions are tied at the end of regulation. After battling to a 28-28 tie after four quarters, they go to midfield for a coin toss before starting overtime. The Bucs win the toss and elect to go on offense.

The game has been wide open all night, and the teams continue to play in that style. On the first play in overtime the Bucs are passing, but the Lions are ready and their cornerback makes an interception. He fumbles the ball, however, and the Bucs recover.

Whose ball is it? What is your ruling?

### CASE 11: Halftime Intermission

The Bobcats marching band is one of the best in Florida. On homecoming night, they're looking to rock the house at halftime. The Bobcats' home management notifies you, your officiating crew and the coach of the visiting team 30 minutes before game time that the halftime intermission will be extended to accommodate the Bouncing Bobcats band.

Do you allow halftime intermission to be extended? What is your ruling?

### CASE 12: Referee Starts or Stops Clock

Time is running out, the Rockers are trailing, and they are on offense. One more score ties the game, and the quarterback is desperate to stop the clock. He lines up in shotgun formation, 3 yards behind center, and intentionally spikes the ball.

Has a foul been committed? What is your ruling?

### CASE 13: Substitutions

The Blue Devils coach loves to substitute on offense. He's been shuffling players in and out all night, partly to keep them fresh and partly to keep the defense guessing.

The Blue Devils obviously spend a lot of time practicing substitutions and knowing what personnel is supposed to be in the game for given situations, because there has been little confusion all game. But late in the third quarter one of the Blue Devils flankers forgets to go in the game. After his team lines up, the flanker notices that only 10 players are on the field. He suddenly remembers that he is supposed to be on the field and dashes into position just before the ball is snapped. He gets set before the ball is snapped and is in his legal position. Has the flanker fouled up? What is your ruling?

# Rule 4: Ball in Play, Dead Ball and Out of Bounds

Rule 4 details what actions to take when deciding whether the ball is still in play, whether it is a dead ball or whether it is indeed out of bounds. The Rule 4 cases we quiz you on include what to do when a live ball strikes an official, when there is an inadvertent whistle, when a holder has his knee on the ground and when a fair-catch signal is given.

### CASE 14: Live Ball Strikes Official

You are lined up in position, right where you are supposed to be as an official, yet something embarrassing is about to happen. You are about to become part of the play.

You are in the defensive zone, and the quarterback fires a pass toward a receiver, but it's coming right at you. You cannot avoid the ball. It caroms off your body and stays airborne, and an eligible receiver catches it in the air. You might be red-faced, but you still have to make the call. Is it a reception? What is your ruling?

### CASE 15: Inadvertent Whistle

On fourth and goal at the 5-yard line, the Zips run an off-tackle play. The tailback fumbles at the line of scrimmage, and the ball squirts into the end zone. As it is rolling into the end zone, you accidentally blow your whistle. An official would like to avoid this situation, but rules are in place to deal with these kinds of mistakes.

The Bearcats defense recovers the ball in the end zone after the inadvertent whistle. Does the ball belong to the Zips or the Bearcats? Where do you spot the ball? What is your ruling?

### CASE 16: Holder With Knee on the Ground

On fourth down the Roadrunners line up in field-goal formation on the 20-yard line. The holder has his knee on the ground as he receives the snap. The fake is on. Instead of placing the ball on the ground for a kick, the holder stays in the same position and immediately flips the ball to the kicker, who scampers in for a touchdown. Is it a touchdown?

### CASE 17: Fair-Catch Signal

The Wildcats speedy punt returner is lined up at his own 10-yard line, waiting on a booming spiral. He makes a legal fair-catch signal but muffs the catch. The ball squirts loose, and another Wildcat picks up the ball at the 1-yard line. His momentum carries him into the end zone, where he is tackled.

Is it a safety? Is it a touchback? Or is it the Wildcats' ball at the 1?

# Answers

Here you can check your answers to the cases presented in this chapter.

### Case 1: Number of Players

The Mustangs are left with only nine players. Should the game continue? The answer is yes. Both teams must have 11 players to start the game, but the game can continue even though one team has fewer than 11. A team that has fewer than 11 players receives no penalty, except that when that team is on offense, at least 7 players must be on the line of scrimmage. If a team has fewer than seven players on the field when it is on offense, it may not put the ball in play and, therefore, must forfeit the game.

### Case 2: Teams Entering the Field

The Cougars may be at home and want to get that last cheer, but the referee should order the home team to enter the field first. The rules do not specifically cover this situation, so the referee uses his discretion.

### Case 3: Choice of Ball

Requests 1, 2 and 3 should be denied. Request 4 should be granted. Officials can grant a request to change from rubber to leather or vice versa only for a free kick or to start a series. If weather conditions warrant a switch (which they didn't in this case), the officials can make a switch from one leather ball to another or from one rubber ball to another within a series.

### Case 4: Legal and Illegal Equipment

The coach was sharp enough to get the signed medical form. Without it, the cornerback could not wear the device during the game. But the medical form makes it OK.

### Case 5: Video Replays

Sorry, Tigers, not in high school. Game officials cannot use video monitoring or replay equipment to make any decision relating to the game.

### Case 6: Legal and Illegal Blocking

The Bears offensive tackle has made a legal block, even though at one point he is blocking in the back. Here's why: His original block was legal, and his contact in the back was simply a continuation of that legal block. As long as the initial block was legal and contact continues, the Bears tackle is within the rules. The extended-arm, open-hand technique is always legal.

### Case 7: Catching the Ball

The Pirates' passing game scores again. As long as the ball doesn't touch the ground, it is perfectly legal for two (or more) receivers to touch it before one of them gains possession. The touchdown stands.

### Case 8: Conference

The Shamrocks head coach has done nothing illegal by entering the midfield conference, wearing a headset or communicating with an assistant on the sideline. Players, however, are not allowed to communicate on the headset. But because this didn't occur, no violation has been committed.

### Case 9: Pass or Fumble?

A tough night for the quarterback just got tougher. Because his arm had not yet begun the forward motion when he lost control of the ball, it is a fumble.

### Case 10: Resolving Tied Games

When all the action ended, the Bucs had the ball. But they turn it over anyway. Because the game was in overtime, the ball was dead as soon as the Lions made the interception. Although the Bucs recovered a fumble after the interception, it was a dead ball. The Lions will put the ball in play to start their series of four downs, first and goal from the 10-yard line.

### Case 11: Halftime Intermission

The Bobcats band might want to bounce all night on homecoming, but the rules restrict the length of halftime intermission to 20 minutes. Neither

It is legal for a pass to be touched by two or more receivers as long as the receivers are inbounds and the ball does not touch the ground.

mutual agreement nor prior notification can extend intermission. On a side note, if both coaches agree, halftime may be reduced to a minimum of 10 minutes.

### Case 12: Referee Starts or Stops Clock

The quarterback has made a mistake. A quarterback can intentionally spike the ball if he takes a direct hand-to-hand snap. But the quarterback was in shotgun formation, 3 yards behind center. Because he intentionally spiked the ball after receiving something other than a hand-to-hand snap, he has thrown an illegal forward pass and his team will be penalized.

### Case 13: Substitutions
The Blue Devils forgetful flanker has committed no foul provided his coming onto the field late was not viewed as an attempt to deceive the defense and if he did not violate shift or motion provisions, was on his side of the neutral zone and was within 15 yards of the ball. The flanker may have drawn the ire of his coach, but he drew no penalty flag on this play.

### Case 14: Live Ball Strikes Official
An official struck by a pass in play may suffer embarrassment, but that doesn't alter the status of the play. In this case, the ball stayed in the air, and an eligible receiver caught it. It is a reception.

### Case 15: Inadvertent Whistle
By being prepared to deal with these kinds of situations, you can minimize embarrassment and quickly heal any damage to your credibility. In this case, the inadvertent whistle occurred while the play was in progress. The Zips have the choice of either accepting the ball at the spot of the fumble (the 5-yard line) or replaying the down. In either case, the Bearcats will be angry because they recovered the fumble after your inadvertent whistle. But regardless of consequence, you must follow the rule.

### Case 16: Holder With Knee on the Ground
Because the knee of the Roadrunners holder was still on the ground when he flipped the ball to the kicker for a run, the ball is immediately a dead ball, and the ball is turned over on downs. If the holder had risen off his knee before making the pitch, the play would have been valid.

### Case 17: Fair-Catch Signal
The Wildcats return man didn't catch the punt, but his team catches a break, in a manner of speaking. After a muffed return, the ball is dead as soon as it is recovered, no matter who makes the recovery. So the returner was bailed out by his teammate, who recovered at the 1. Momentum, incidentally, is irrelevant after a muff. No return is allowed, regardless of who recovers. The ball is a dead ball on recovery.

# PLAY

The fun continues in this chapter. As in chapter 5, we are going to bring some situations to life for you, action that you might face during a game. Then we will let you decide what ruling to make. We will present scenarios dealing with a series of rules, and then at the end of the chapter, we will give you the ruling you should have made.

In chapter 6, we'll present rulings for the next four rules:

- Rule 5: Series of Downs, Number of Down and Team Possession After Penalties
- Rule 6: Kicking the Ball and Fair Catch
- Rule 7: Snapping, Handing and Passing the Ball
- Rule 8: Scoring Plays and Touchbacks

Remember, first we will give you the scenarios and situations. The answers appear at the end of the chapter. The game has begun. Make your rulings. Try to make your calls quickly and decisively, to simulate a game situation as closely as possible.

## Rule 5: Series of Downs, Number of Down and Team Possession After Penalties

Rule 5 details protocol to follow concerning a series of downs, the number of the down and team possession after penalties. The Rule 5 cases we quiz you on include incorrect down, the effect of a receiving team touching a kick and ball position during measurement. Consider how you'd respond in each situation and check your judgments against the answers beginning on page 138 at the end of the chapter.

### CASE 1: Incorrect Down
The game has been wild. The Blazers like to run the hurry-up offense, a rarity in high school football, and their play has given the game an

entirely different rhythm than what you're used to. At one point in the confusion, you realize that the Blazers just ran a fifth-down play. That's right. Fifth down.

What do you do to correct the situation? What is your ruling?

### CASE 2: Effect of Receiving Team Touching Kick

The Mules are down by two points late in the game. The Mules kicker already has kicked three long field goals, so it's no surprise when he comes out to try a 35-yarder that might win the game.

A Spartans defender blocks the kick, however, and a scramble for the ball ensues. A Spartan has a bead on the ball, which has gone beyond the neutral zone, but muffs it in his attempt to gain possession. The Mules then recover the ball.

Whose ball is it? What is your ruling?

### CASE 3: Ball Position During Measurement

It's fourth and 1 in a critical situation. The Panthers quarterback tries a sneak up the middle to gain the yard. He is extremely close to the first down, but you notice that the ball comes down parallel to the yard line. You realize that if you order a measurement with the ball that way, it will not be a first down. But if you turn the ball so that it is parallel to the sideline, a first down will result.

Do you change position of the ball before the measurement? What is your ruling?

# Rule 6: Kicking the Ball and Fair Catch

Rule 6 details some examples of what can happen during the kicking game, including the actual kicking of the ball and fair-catch complications. The Rule 6 cases we quiz you on include simultaneous recovery, blocking a kick from the crossbar, kicking into a receiving team's end zone and an invalid signal. Consider how you'd respond in each situation and check your judgments against the answers beginning on page 139 at the end of the chapter.

### CASE 4: Simultaneous Recovery

On fourth and 3 at their own 10-yard line, the Saints go into punting formation. The Demons block the kick, and the ball squirts into the end zone. A Demon and a Saint each dive on the ball and recover it at the same moment. You determine that it is simultaneous possession.

Is it a touchback? A safety? A touchdown for the Demons? What is your ruling?

### CASE 5: Blocking Kick From Crossbar

The Lancers have a player who also plays basketball. He's quite a leaper, so the coach puts him in the end zone when opponents are trying field goals. His job is to stand under the crossbar and jump up to block the field goal. The play rarely works, but—lucky you—it does tonight. The Lancers leaper jumps up and blocks the ball away from the crossbar.

Is this a legal play? If so, where do you place the ball? What is your ruling?

### CASE 6: Kicks Into Receiving Team's End Zone

The Niners punt from midfield. The punt is a high spiral that gives their players time to get down near the goal line when the ball lands at the Falcons' 5-yard line. After it lands, the ball takes a huge bounce and a Niners player leaps, gains possession in the air at the 1-yard line and then lands in the end zone.

Many unique circumstances can occur during a kicking down that test the officials' mastery of the rules.

Does the ball belong to the Falcons at the 1-yard line? Or is it a touchback? What is your ruling?

### CASE 7: Invalid Signal

The Patriots are facing fourth and 6 at their own 9-yard line, so they go back to punt. The kick is awful—very high and very short. The Zips return man races up to try to catch the ball in the neutral zone. He's running hard and trying to make a fair-catch signal at the same time.

The signal by the Zips return man is barely perceptible, and he is flagged for making an invalid signal. He never does make it to the ball, which lands untouched and rebounds behind the neutral zone. The Patriots recover the ball and are downed at their own 8.

Has a foul been committed? Where do you spot the ball? Who gains possession? What is your ruling?

# Rule 7: Snapping, Handing and Passing the Ball

Rule 7 details the different kind of violations that can occur when snapping, handing off or passing the football. The Rule 7 cases we quiz you on include snap techniques, handoffs and passing in the neutral zone. Consider how you'd respond in each situation and check your judgments against the answers beginning on page 139 at the end of the chapter.

### CASE 8: Snap Techniques

The Chiefs center feels more comfortable snapping the ball from a 90-degree angle. So before the snap, he makes preliminary adjustments to tilt the ball at that angle.

Is this a legal adjustment? What is your ruling?

### CASE 9: Handoffs

The Hawks quarterback has been running wild all night. He's tricky with handoffs and fake handoffs, and he has been keeping the Lions off balance all game.

The quarterback sees an opening around the right side and takes off running. Just after crossing the neutral zone, he sees that he's about to be hit. His tailback sees what is happening and comes close to him to receive a handoff. The quarterback hands the ball off, but you determine that the handoff went forward. The quarterback did not pitch the ball; he made a direct hand-to-hand exchange. But the handoff was definitely forward, and it occurred beyond the neutral zone.

Is this a legal handoff? What is your ruling?

### CASE 10: Passing in the Neutral Zone

The Chargers quarterback has been lighting up the Cougars all night, but on this play he's running for his life from the Cougars defensive end. The quarterback outwits the defensive end with a deke move, but the defensive end is closing in for the hit. The quarterback scrambles toward the neutral zone and gets rid of the ball. As he releases the pass, his foremost foot is on the ground and is barely breaking the plane of the neutral zone.

Has the quarterback thrown an illegal pass? What is your ruling?

# Rule 8: Scoring Plays and Touchbacks

Rule 8 details what actions to take when deciding whether the ball is still in play, whether it is a dead ball or whether it is indeed out of bounds. The Rule 8 cases we quiz you on include what to do during and after point-after-touchdown plays, fumbles in the end zone and field goals. Consider how you'd respond in each situation and check your judgments against the answers beginning on page 140 at the end of the chapter.

Top officials watch a play and anticipate the types of situations that might occur, rather than reacting after the play's completion.

### CASE 11: Point After Touchdown

The Shamrocks are up by 38 points late in the fourth quarter and they score another touchdown on a long run to put them up by 44. The Shamrocks coach doesn't want to rub it in, so he tells his captain to inform you that they don't want to attempt a point-after-touchdown play.

Do you force them to make the attempt anyway? What is your ruling?

### CASE 12: Fumble in End Zone on Kickoff

The Panthers kick off to the Bobcats to start the second half, and the Bobcats return man is running free toward the end zone. But at the last second a Panthers player dives and knocks the ball out of the return man's hands at the 5-yard line. The ball rolls into the end zone, but for some reason neither team makes a move to recover it.

The ball just sits there, with players from both teams surrounding it, unsure of what to do. Do you blow the whistle? Is it a touchdown? A touchback? What is your ruling?

### CASE 13: Field Goals

A Chargers player lines up for a potential game-winning field goal. The kick is from 35 yards in the rain—a long kick but within the player's range. A successful kick will knock the Cougars from the playoffs. The player boots the ball and the kick hugs the left upright and has plenty of distance. So much distance, in fact, that it goes above the upright.

You determine that the ball went directly above the left upright. Is it a successful field goal, or do the Cougars make the playoffs? What is your ruling?

# Answers

Here you can check your answers to the cases presented in this chapter.

### Case 1: Incorrect Down

The good thing is that you realized your mistake, which was that you allowed the Blazers to run a down when they should have turned the ball over. But the key to correcting the situation is this: When did you make the discovery that they had run too many downs? If you realized the error before you awarded a new series, then play reverts to where it was before the fifth down was run. But once you've awarded a new series, the play stands.

### Case 2: Effect of Receiving Team Touching Kick

The Mules catch a break here. Their kick was blocked, but because the Spartans muffed the recovery attempt beyond the neutral zone and the Mules then recovered, the Mules take possession. If the Mules recover the muff behind the neutral zone, they can advance the ball. If they recover beyond the neutral zone, they cannot advance it. But in either case, they take possession.

### Case 3: Ball Position During Measurement

Regardless of the effect that the position of the ball will have on the measurement, you must position the ball so that it is parallel to the sideline when ordering a measurement. Remember that the farthest point of the ball must stay in the same position. The rule allows no exceptions.

### Case 4: Simultaneous Recovery

This is a touchdown for the Demons. In simultaneous possession, the receiving team is granted possession by rule.

### Case 5: Blocking Kick From Crossbar

This is a legal play. If an athlete can leap above the crossbar to block a kick, it's within the rules. In this case, a touchback results, and the Lancers take possession at their own 20-yard line.

### Case 6: Kicks Into Receiving Team's End Zone

This play results in a touchback, and the Falcons take possession at their own 20-yard line. Although the Niners player controlled the ball at the 1-yard line, he does not complete the recovery until he lands inbounds with the ball in his possession. Because he lands in the end zone, it is a touchback.

### Case 7: Invalid Signal

The Zips returner has committed a foul for an invalid signal even though he never got to the ball. The Patriots undoubtedly will accept this penalty because instead of giving the ball to the Zips, the Patriots keep possession with a fourth and 1 from 14.

### Case 8: Snap Techniques

The Chiefs center has done nothing illegal by tilting the ball to 90 degrees. If, however, he had lifted the ball and pushed it forward on a deep snap, rotated the ball end for end, or removed both hands from the ball and then replaced them, a dead-ball, 5-yard penalty would be the correct call.

### Case 9: Handoffs

The Hawks quarterback committed a foul. Although he made a hand-to-hand exchange, he cannot hand the ball forward if the ball has passed the neutral zone. The position of the ball (not the players) determines whether the handoff is beyond the neutral zone. If the entire ball is beyond the neutral zone when the exchange occurs, then the handoff is forward.

### Case 10: Passing in the Neutral Zone

The Chargers quarterback might have been having a good night passing, but on this play he strayed from the rules. If any part of a quarterback's body breaks the plane of the neutral zone before he releases the ball, the forward pass is illegal. The Cougars defensive end might have avoided a sack, but he picked up a penalty.

### Case 11: Point After Touchdown

The Shamrocks coach made a sporting gesture, but he has no choice. You must force the Shamrocks to attempt the try, or at least snap the ball.

### Case 12: Fumble in End Zone on Kickoff

This play may be confusing for the players, but it shouldn't be confusing for you. After waiting a few seconds, the referee should sound the whistle and signal a touchdown. If no one makes a move to recover, then the fumbling team retains possession. Because the Bobcats had last possession and the ball is in the Panthers' end zone, a touchdown is the result.

### Case 13: Field Goals

The Cougars are in the playoffs. The Chargers' kick was plenty long, but if you rule that it went directly over the upright, the kick is unsuccessful. The ball must penetrate the plane of the goal between the insides of the uprights extended.

# CHAPTER 7

# KEEPING IT FAIR

In this chapter, we deal first with the most emotionally charged situations an official might face. In most cases, conduct of players and coaches should not be a chronic issue, but even so, you need to know how to react properly to an occasional flare-up.

Officials can keep unsporting conduct penalties, personal fouls and disqualifications to a minimum by preemptive communication throughout the game. "Hey, twenty-four, watch that" is a simple way of preventing number 24 from thinking that he can get away with something that might result in an opponent's retaliation and escalation into a messy scene.

A good official has a feel for the game and recognizes when things are getting out of hand. Do your best to prevent situations that call for disqualifications and flagrant-foul penalties. Sometimes, however, you cannot foresee the occurrence of confrontational situations because they result from heat-of-the-moment decisions made by emotional coaches or young athletes. In the first portion of this chapter, under Rule 9, we deal with sample scenarios of misconduct and ask you to make a ruling. In the Rule 10 portion of this chapter, we ask you about situations that call for enforcement of penalties in a variety of situations. You will find the answers to these situations at the end of the chapter.

## Rule 9: Conduct of Players and Others

Rule 9 details what actions to take when emotions run high and the conduct of players, coaches and others threatens to become inappropriate. The Rule 9 cases we quiz you on include situations involving fighting, a flagrant foul, whether a player is roughing the passer and what to do when a coach's conduct is in question. Consider how you'd respond in each situation and check your judgments against the answers beginning on page 144 at the end of the chapter.

### CASE 1: Fighting
The Ravens and the Bisons are two of the roughest teams in your area, and they've lived up to their reputations on this night. The game generally

has been toughly contested throughout, with a few minor skirmishes. That changes quickly after a play on the Ravens' 2-yard line.

A full-scale fight involving two players breaks out. Both players throw punches, but no official saw which player threw the first punch.

Is one player disqualified? Two players? How do you enforce deadball penalties? What is your ruling?

### CASE 2: Flagrant Foul

The Rams tailback streaks in for a touchdown on a sweep play from the 10-yard line. Time is running out, and the score puts the Rams up by three touchdowns on the Falcons, clearly sealing the outcome of the game.

Knowing this and feeling frustrated, a Falcons defender takes a cheap, blindside shot at the Rams quarterback well behind the play. You rule that the contact was not only unnecessarily rough but also flagrant.

Is there a penalty? A disqualification? What is your ruling?

### CASE 3: Roughing the Passer

The Eagles quarterback is both a skilled football player and a gifted trash talker. He's been shredding the Raiders' defense all night, and he's also

A single unsportsmanlike act can change the tenor of the game. Use preventative measures when possible, but penalize when necessary.

been letting them know about it. The Raiders 290-pound defensive tackle has been chasing the Eagles quarterback all night (with little success) and has had enough.

The Eagles quarterback rolls out to the Raiders defensive tackle's side of the field, unknowingly crosses the line of scrimmage and lets go a pass. The defensive tackle knows that the quarterback has released the pass and he could have stopped his charge, but is frustrated and lets loose on him anyway. The shot isn't to the head, or with a forearm or anything that ordinarily would be considered flagrant. But it is a solid shot after the quarterback had released the ball.

Is the Raiders defensive tackle guilty of roughing the passer? What is your ruling?

### CASE 4: Coach's Conduct

A coach had received an unsporting-conduct penalty earlier in the game, but that is not deterring him during a vehement argument in the middle of the third quarter. You rule that the coach has stepped over the line again, and issue him another unsporting foul.

Because the foul is the coach's second unsporting foul of the game, you inform him that he may no longer remain in the vicinity of the playing field and that he may not have any contact with his players, either direct or indirect, throughout the remainder of the game.

Can the coach go to the stands? The press box? The team locker room? What is your ruling?

# Rule 10: Enforcement of Penalties

Rule 10 details the procedures to take when a penalty has been called and the procedures to use in enforcing penalties. The Rule 10 cases we quiz you on include what to do when there is a double foul, how to spot the ball for enforcement, how to handle a foul during a scoring play and special enforcements. Consider how you'd respond in each situation and check your judgments against the answers beginning on page 146 at the end of the chapter.

### CASE 5: Double Fouls

The Blazers tailback has beaten the Wolverines defense and is streaking down the sideline when he loses the football. Before the fumble, one of the Blazers linemen was flagged for offensive holding. While the teams are scrambling for the football, a Wolverine grasps and twists a Blazer facemask. Meanwhile, a Wolverine picks up the ball and runs for a touchdown.

Where do you spot the ball? Whose ball is it? Is it a touchdown? What is your ruling?

### CASE 6: Basic Enforcement Spots
Student-body right has been working all game for the Lakers, so they go to the well one more time. On a sweep-pitch play from the Jets' 40-yard line, the Lakers halfback finds a seam and scampers 30 yards to the Jets' 10. During the pitch, a Jets defender is called for holding at his own 22.

From what point would you enforce the penalty if the Lakers accept it? What is your ruling?

### CASE 7: Foul During Scoring Play
The Golden Bears hold a 16-7 lead over the Sharks with four minutes left in the game. On third and 9 from their own 19, the Golden Bears staff elects to try a pass. The call is curious, given the game situation, and it becomes more alarming when the quarterback scrambles backward to his own end zone and releases a wild pass. While the quarterback is in the end zone, one of his linemen is called for holding. The quarterback's pass is intercepted and returned for a touchdown.

The Sharks want to turn down the score, however, and accept the holding penalty in the end zone. The penalty would result in a safety and a free kick to the Sharks, which would give them an opportunity to score the winning touchdown. Wade through the confusion.

What is your ruling?

### CASE 8: Special Enforcements
The Hurons are on offense and snap the ball just before time expires at the end of the first half. As the Hurons quarterback scrambles, time expires and he is tackled in the end zone before he can get a pass away. During the down, a Hurons lineman is called for holding in the end zone.

Is it a safety? If so, do the Hurons have to execute a free kick to the Bolts before halftime? Does the penalty in the end zone have a bearing on either of these decisions? What is your ruling?

# Answers

Here you can check your answers to the cases presented in this chapter.

### Case 1: Fighting
Both players in the fight are disqualified because officials saw each throwing a punch. But because no official saw who threw the first punch, you don't know in which order you should enforce the 15-yard penalties. You can't randomly enforce them because with the ball at the 2-yard line, you would mark off only half the distance to the goal in one direction. Because you have no way to prevent an inequity, you enforce no yardage penalties.

### Case 2: Flagrant Foul

Occasionally, if a team scores a touchdown and what otherwise would be called a flagrant defensive foul occurs on the play, officials might overlook the foul because the offensive team scored a touchdown anyway. Avoid this temptation! A flagrant foul is a flagrant foul. The touchdown counts, the defensive player is disqualified because the foul was deemed flagrant and the penalty is enforced on the succeeding spot.

### Case 3: Roughing the Passer

The Raiders defensive tackle gets away with one here. The trash-talking Eagles quarterback lost his special protection as a passer when he passed the line of scrimmage. Even if the defensive tackle had no idea that the quarterback had passed the line, you don't penalize him because he is a runner after he passes the line.

### Case 4: Coach's Conduct

Following his ejection from the premises, the coach is free to continue venting in the team locker room, but he may not stay in the stands or the

Knowing the type of play in which a foul occurred, such as running or loose-ball play, is key to proper penalty enforcement.

press box. Had the coach's ejection occurred in the first half, however, he would have had to leave the locker room during halftime and would have been free to return to the locker room only after the players had left to start the third quarter.

### Case 5: Double Fouls

This play between the Blazers and the Wolverines includes plenty of action—two penalties, a fumble and a touchdown—but it's all coming back. Because both penalties occurred before the change of team possession, a double foul is the correct call. Therefore, the penalties cancel, and the down is replayed.

### Case 6: Basic Enforcement Spots

Holding by the Jets defender occurred during a loose-ball play, so the penalty would be enforced from the previous spot. In this case, that would be the Jets' 40. Because the Lakers sweep resulted in a gain to the Jets' 10, obviously they would refuse the penalty.

### Case 7: Foul During Scoring Play

The Sharks are within their rights to turn down the touchdown and accept the penalty. Doing so makes sense because they would have a better chance to win the game after receiving a free kick. If the Sharks want to decline holding on the Golden Bears, they may.

### Case 8: Special Enforcements

Regardless of whether the Bolts accept the penalty, the result of the play is a safety against the Hurons. If the Bolts accept the penalty, the Hurons must execute a free kick to the Bolts with an untimed down before the half ends. Almost certainly, under these conditions, the Bolts would accept the penalty to have a chance at a kick return.

## NFHS Officiating Football Signals

Ball ready for play;
untimed down

Start clock

Time-out

TV/radio time-out

Touchdown; field goal;
point(s) after touchdown

Safety

Dead-ball foul; touchback
(move side to side)

First down

Loss of down

Incomplete forward pass;
penalty declined; no play; no
score; toss option delayed

Legal touching of
forward pass or
scrimmage kick

Inadvertent whistle
(face press box)

Disregard flag

End of period

Sideline warning

First touching (NFHS); illegal touching

Uncatchable forward pass (NCAA only)

Encroachment (NFHS); offside defense (NCAA)

Illegal procedure (NFHS); false start; illegal formation; encroachment offense (NCAA)

a

b

(a) Illegal shift and (b) illegal motion

Delay of game

Illegal substitution

Failure to wear required equipment

Illegal
helmet contact

Unsportsmanlike conduct;
noncontact foul

Illegal participation

Sideline interference

Running into or
roughing kicker or holder

Illegal batting

Invalid fair catch (NFHS);
illegal fair catch

Forward-pass interference;
kick-catching interference

Roughing passer

Illegal pass/
forward handing

Intentional grounding

Ineligible downfield
on pass

Personal foul

Clipping

Blocking below waist;
illegal block

Chop block

Holding/obstructing;
illegal use of hands/arms

Illegal block
in the back

Helping runner;
interlocked blocking

Grasping face mask
or helmet opening

Tripping

Player disqualification

# GLOSSARY

**balanced formation**—An offensive formation in which three linemen are on either side of the snapper.

**ball carrier**—The player in possession of the ball. Also known as the runner.

**dead-ball officiating**—Activity during the time immediately after the ball becomes dead. Good dead-ball officials don't stop officiating when the ball is dead. They continue to watch the players and prevent problems.

**downfield**—Refers to the direction the offensive team is moving with the ball. On a scrimmage down, it is the area beyond the neutral zone. Opposite of upfield.

**flat**—The area behind the offensive linemen where backs go to receive short passes. A pass to a back in the flat is thrown shortly after the snap, thus making it different from a screen pass.

**free kick**—A kick from a tee that starts either half or follows a score. A kickoff is a free kick.

**hash marks**—Also known as the inbounds marks, the lines on the field from which the ball is snapped if it becomes dead in a side zone or out of bounds.

**key**—An action or reaction by a player that gives the official a tip about what type of play the offense will run; a player an official observes for all or part of a down.

**line-to-gain crew**—Assistant officials in charge of the line-to-gain equipment. Sometimes referred to as the chain crew.

**line-to-gain equipment**—A 10-yard length of chain connected at each end to poles used to indicate the line the offensive team must reach to achieve a first down. Commonly referred to as the chains.

**NFHS**—Acronym for the National Federation of State High School Associations. The NFHS is the governing body for high school athletics.

**no-call**—A conscious decision by the official that an action was not worthy of a penalty.

**onside kick**—A free kick intentionally kicked a short distance in the hope of recovering the ball. Not to be confused with a squib kick.

**pick play**—Pass play on which one receiver runs a short route, drawing coverage from a defender, and another receiver runs a slightly deeper route. The receiver on the shorter route blocks an opponent, freeing his teammate from coverage. The act is illegal if a forward pass crosses the neutral zone after the block has been thrown.

**pitchout**—A backward pass, usually thrown by the quarterback to a running back.

**place kick**—A kick in which the ball is placed on a tee or held by a teammate.

**point of attack**—On a running play, the area in advance of the runner through which he runs; on a passing play, anywhere near the passer or any player attempting to reach the passer; on a kick play, anywhere near the kicker or any player attempting reach the kicker or block the kick.

**preventive officiating**—Refers to actions by officials who prevent problems from occurring by talking to players and coaches. Preventive officiating is often related to dead-ball officiating.

**pulling**—Tactic by offensive linemen used especially on sweeps. After the snap, a pulling lineman moves quickly from his normal position toward the end of the line or the opposite side of the formation to block an opponent.

**scrimmage kick**—A kick made from scrimmage that precedes a change of team possession. Punts, field goals and kick trys are scrimmage kicks.

**short side**—The side of the field from the hash mark to the nearer sideline when the ball is snapped from the hash mark; opposite of wide side.

**shotgun**—An offensive formation in which the quarterback is several yards behind the snapper.

**side zone**—The area of the field between the sidelines and the hash marks.

**squib kick**—A free kick, usually low and short, kicked to prevent a good return man from returning the kick.

**strong side**—The side of the offensive line on which there are more eligible receivers outside of the tackles; opposite of the weak side.

**trips**—An offensive formation with three eligible receivers on one side.

**weak side**—The side of the offensive line on which there are fewer eligible receivers outside of the tackles; opposite of the strong side.

**wideout**—An eligible receiver who lines up outside the last player on the offensive line, on the line of scrimmage.

**wide side**—The area from the opposite hash mark through the middle of the field and side zone to the sideline when the ball is snapped from the opposite hash mark; opposite of short side.

*Note:* The italicized *f* following page numbers refers to figures.

# ABOUT THE AUTHOR

*Officiating Football* was written by the American Sport Education Program (ASEP) in cooperation with the National Federation of State High School Associations (NFHS). Based in Indianapolis, the NFHS is the rules authority for high school sports in the United States. Hundreds of thousands of officials nationwide and worldwide rely on the NFHS for officiating guidance. ASEP is a division of Human Kinetics, based in Champaign, Illinois, and has been a world leader in providing educational courses and resources to professional and volunteer coaches, officials, parents, and sport administrators for more than 20 years. ASEP and the NFHS have teamed up to offer courses for high school officials through the NFHS Officials Education Program.

# NFHS Officials Education Program

## ONLINE EDUCATION FOR ON-THE-GO OFFICIALS

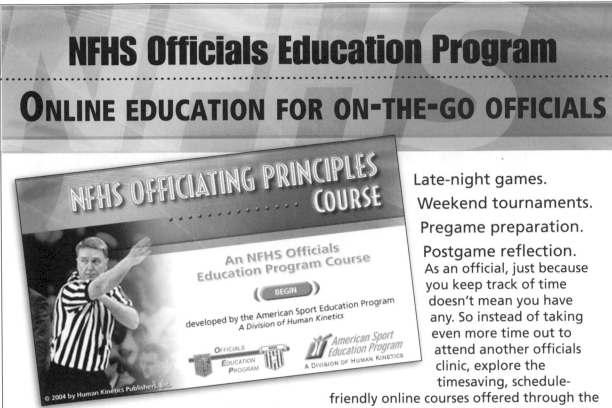

Late-night games.

Weekend tournaments.

Pregame preparation.

Postgame reflection.
As an official, just because you keep track of time doesn't mean you have any. So instead of taking even more time out to attend another officials clinic, explore the timesaving, schedule-friendly online courses offered through the **NFHS Officials Education Program.**

A joint effort between the **National Federation of State High School Associations (NFHS)** and the **American Sport Education Program (ASEP),** the NFHS Officials Education Program features a two-part, Internet-delivered curriculum covering officiating principles and sport-specific methods based on NFHS rules.

Available now is *NFHS Officiating Principles,* a course applicable to all officials regardless of their sport. The course shows you how to determine your officiating philosophy and style, improve communication, develop decision-making skills, manage conflict, understand legal responsibilities, manage your officiating career, and much more.

Coming soon: *Officiating [Sport] Methods* courses for softball, football, soccer, basketball, wrestling, and baseball cover the sport-specific methods and mechanics of officiating as they apply to NFHS rules and regulations. The officiating [sport] book that you have in your hands serves as the text for the course. Check the ASEP Web site at www.ASEP.com for updates on course availability.

NFHS Officials Education Program offers you the continuing education you need as an official on a schedule that's right for you. Registration fees are only $75 per course and include a course text, CD-ROM, study guide, exam, and entry into the National Officials Registry. For more information, or to register for a course, visit **www.ASEP.com** or call ASEP at **800-747-5698.**

WITHDRAWN

Emory & Henry College
Emory, VA 24327

3  1836  0022  6862  1